Social Organization:
Symbol, Structure,
and Setting

Social Organization: Symbol, Structure, and Setting

Henry A. Selby

Temple University

WM. C. BROWN COMPANY PUBLISHERS

Dubuque, Iowa

ANTHROPOLOGY SERIES

Consulting Editors

Frank Johnston
University of Pennsylvania

Henry Selby
Temple University

Contents

Preface

This book is intended for beginning students in anthropology. I have tried to set down my best idea of what anthropologists are presently thinking about when they deal with social organization. I should probably warn teachers (who do not need the warning since they can flip through the pages and see for themselves) that it is not exactly a standard treatment. It is not intended to replace lectures or textbooks, but rather to supplement them. I have included a lot of *motivating* material, topics that have appealed to my students in the past and persuaded them that the subject has a broader appeal than merely the study of what used to be called "primitive social organization." Some topics (like the analysis of kinship terminologies) are omitted because practically all textbooks and most lecturers give perfectly adequate information on the subject.

The book is based on a course that I have given in various forms to graduates and undergraduates at three universities for the past eight years. I would like to thank the students for their patience and constructive criticism, and in particular thank one Temple University student in Anthropology 21, who stated flatly that it was impossible to take notes from me, and why didn't I write this stuff down in a way that people can understand it! I hope the book meets his standards.

Cape Cod, Massachusetts

1 | Introduction

IS PROGRESS A MYTH?

There are two ways of thinking about the ways human beings organize themselves: one can think of humankind progressing from caveman to commuter, or as it is sometimes put, from savagery to civilization or one can think of the organization of human groups as being a set of answers to problems set by the environment and by human needs for sociability and sustenance. The first way of thinking is *evolutionary*. The argument is that man has evolved from his cave past in the Lower Paleolithic when culture was invented and has steadily increased his capability to organize himself and sustain his body and spirit in increasingly complex and satisfactory ways. And this is a fact. "Cave people" did exist. Culture was invented about 2 to 2.5 million years ago and contemporary humankind does live in altered circumstances.

But, although all anthropologists study our past and two branches of anthropology, paleontology and archeology, are devoted to it, most of us (myself included) find the idea of "progress" hard to swallow. Some people, Leslie White among the most articulate, accept the notion that our ability to create and harness greater amounts of energy is a measure of our evolutionary progress—and it is certainly true that we use up a great deal of energy.

But it this progress? I am writing these pages during a brownout and have been listening to the representatives of the energy industries telling me that I have to accept the "trade-off" between clean air and water and turning on my air conditioner.

Some people point to the great elaboration of our technological inventory and call that evolution. And it is true that our "cave people" of the Lower Paleolithic had a few stone tools and perhaps a throwing stick at their command, whereas we have lasers and computers. But is our measure of progress to be technology? The Arunta tribesmen of the central region of Australia don't have or need two-car garages: their techological inventory consists of boomerangs, clubs, spears, spear throwers, dibbles (digging sticks), netted string bags, a shallow basin made of bark, some stone tools, and that is about it. But they manage. And they manage a lot better in some important ways than we do. They don't worry about taking vacations: they never work unless they have to and that is about half the time (compared to us). They don't worry about father commuting to the city: when he isn't out hunting, he is at home, and he doesn't hunt unless he both *has* to and there *is* game to hunt! Besides this, these "savages" with their incredibly simpleminded technology have a rich and complex kinship system (which we will

1

briefly examine later), a ritual cycle, and a cosmology that in its dimensions and richness beggars the media-ridden conventional wisdom that most of us (including academics and intellectuals) traffic in.

The point of view that I am taking is an extreme form of *cultural relativism*, which means that I don't think that you can compare cultures and say that one is better than another. You can certainly say they are different, and we will be examining some of the differences in this book. But not better.

Some students and other thoughtful people find this at least as hard to swallow as I find the idea of progress hard to digest. A critic could well state: "Look, it's all very well to say that we aren't better than everyone else just because we have all this progress stuff—but what about poverty, starvation, illness, suffering, premature death, disease, and the like? Surely we have made some progress by eliminating these. Isn't it better to be comfortable than uncomfortable, is it not better to be well than ill, rich than poor, full-bellied than starving? Isn't this progress in an *absolute* sense?" And my answer is the usual social science answer "yes-and-no." Take illness and health for an example. Look what we have had to give up for it. We have given the care of our lives over to specialists in their hospitals where they perform curing practices from which we are excluded and over which we have no control. We cannot decide when to die, anymore than when to be born; specialists bring us into the world and they ferry us out of it.[1] But more importantly we don't even understand what goes on in our own bodies. Things have become so complicated, and the jargon of the specialists so difficult to understand, that we don't know how our own bodies work nor what the relationship between our bodies and our minds might be. We do not know why we are depressed, happy, in pain, healthy, self-destructive. We don't

even know how to ask questions about our bodies—if you don't believe this, wait until you have to make the decision about whether to have a serious operation or not. The most disquieting thing about all these decisions is that they are made in a vacuum.

So-called primitive, or preliterate, peoples don't have this problem. They have a theory about their bodies, their souls, their psyches, about happiness, sickness, and depression that explains things to them and places them in the company of all the creatures of the earth.

THE NONEVOLUTIONARY APPROACH

So much for progress. Like everything else it is relative. The way we are going to study human social organization is through the *comparative* study of society. Social organization is the study of *collective behavior*, which is just a fancy term for people-doing-things-together. Anthropologists go far and wide in their travels and know how people organize themselves all over the world, and this book is an introduction to that enterprise in understanding. But the book isn't going to be a jumble of anecdotes about the clever ways in which the traditional peoples of the world organize themselves. It is going to be logically organized, starting with the simplest units and ending up with the most complex. And the reason for my rather extended discussion about evolution is that I do not want the reader to get

---

1. Professor Robert Fulton, a sociologist who heads the Center for Death Education at the University of Minnesota, was recently (July 21, 1974) quoted in the New York Times as stating that in a recent study of 560 cases of bereaved persons, "in most cases no family members were present at the death bed, and most of the survivors learned of the death by a telephone call from a nurse, secretary, or other stranger."

into thinking that I am talking about progress. I am talking about the *logical ordering* of our ideas about social organization.

THREE THEMES

There will be three themes that I am going to emphasize in this book; the *structure* of groups, or how they are put together; the *semiotics* of social organization, or the meanings that we commit ourselves to when we organize ourselves in a specific way; and, finally, the *ecology* of human social organization, or the way human beings shape their environment and are affected by it.

The structure of groups means the way they are put together: the parts that make up the whole and the design of parts and the whole. If you want the best possible car in the world you do not take the engine of a Mercedes, the body of a Ferrari, the suspension of a Jaguar, and the chrome from a Pontiac, and put them together, even though some people might advise you that Mercedes' engines were best, Ferrari's bodies were without peer, and so on. The car would look as though it were designed by a committee and probably wouldn't work at all, because the parts have to be designed to fit together, and when you get the right parts together you have more than a bunch of parts: you have an automobile. This is one way of looking at society: discovering what the parts are, how they fit together, and how the whole is designed. Sometimes this approach is called the "structural-functional" approach emphasizing that one has to study more than the shape or the form of the parts; one must also examine the function that each part plays in the working whole. The person who described the carburetor as "the thingamajig that takes in the gas, mixes it with air, and sends it to the cylinder heads" clearly didn't describe the form or the structure of the carburetor, but

showed some intuition about its *function*. So it is with society: different parts of society have different roles to play, different functions. Anthropologists have been good at this kind of analysis because the people they usually study are different and exotic and difficult to understand. As a result anthropologists draw the broad outlines of society; that is, they explain the design of the whole and, in that context, discuss the parts and their structure and function.

The semiotic aspect of social organization refers to *meaning*. *Semiology* is the study of meaning of different codes, including language, but greater than the study of language which is called linguistics. As Roland Barthes pointed out, a menu is a kind of code. It has a structure of meaning: certain courses must follow other courses, you don't serve the soup last in a five course dinner, and you don't put tomato ketchup in the salad, even though you might well serve a broth made from coffee beans last and put tomatoes in the salad. It is a characteristic of human beings to attach meanings to their social forms and these meanings are very much a part of anthopological inquiry.

The semiotics of social organization also bids us study the implications of the way we organize ourselves for our understanding of each other and the world of meaning that we live in. Let me give you an example from my own experience. I attended a women's liberation meeting some years ago when husbands were invited so that they might understand what their wives were on about. Toward the end of the meeting a well-dressed businessman became quite impatient with the whole proceeding and asked the question that blacks and other minorities in America are so accustomed to: "What do you really want?" A number of goals was enumerated by the women and the businessman's face lit up because now he realized that he

3

could be of some assistance. "Form committees," he said, "elect chairmen (sic), get a president and a board of directors, organize task forces, choose your priorities, set your goals, and go after them!" There was a stunned silence, and then one of the members intoned with a patient finality, "we don't do things that way!"

It seems to me that what she was saying was that once you commit yourself to a fragmented, bureaucratic, hierarchical form of social organization you are committing yourself to a set of meanings and values. For one thing the equality upon which the rap group is based is immediately broken down because you have chairpersons and experts and debates over priorities in which individuals come into combative relationships, and you build an organizational ladder just as though you were working for IBM or General Motors. But the point of the rap group is to emphasize the personal, the intimate, the social, the commonality of problems that *all* women share. There are no experts because the purpose of the meeting is understanding. These were the values that were being emphasized, not the efficient organization of human material ("operatives?") so as to attain some goal in the most efficient possible way (maximize profit?). When you organize yourselves in a certain way you commit yourself to a view of the world and a set of meanings and values and exclude others. This is the semiotic aspect of social organization.

The *ecological* aspects of social organization refer to the ways that a society fits into shapes and is constrained by its setting or environment. The important word here is *constrained*. We contrast two ideas: constrain versus determine. No contemporary anthropologist believes that the environment determines the form of the society. If that were the case, then, wher-

ever we found similar environments we would find similar forms of social organization, and this isn't true. To take an obvious example: if we were studying two different environments, one a plain or savannah and the other a highland, mountainous area, it is quite clear that the spread of ideas and "empires" is going to be much easier in the plain than it is in the mountains where each tribal or subtribal grouping is going to be cut off from its neighbors by difficult passes. Similarly, different technologies, which, in turn, are constrained by environments, constrain, in turn, the form of social organizations. To cite the classic example: where irrigation systems require that large numbers of people work together in allocating water to their fields, we are going to find a different form of social organization than where the technology is the basic hunting one we described for the Arunta. Karl Wittofgel suggested, with some truth, that you tend to get centralized, hierarchical forms of government in the first case, and, in the second, you tend to find social organizations that are based on family hunting groups. Environment constrains technology which constrains social organization.

In this book I will tend to discuss form, function, and meaning together and pay only passing attention to ecological factors. In the last chapter I will discuss ecology focusing on a special problem which has interested me and a large number of fellow social scientists: the problem of whether human beings can be said to be rational in the way they organize themselves to fit into their environment and build a decent life for themselves. Even though the book is unbalanced in this way, you should not take this to mean that somehow meaning is subordinate to form and function and that ecological factors are the last to be considered. To understand human social organization we must understand the relationship between all these factors.

Bibliography

Barthes, Roland 1968. *Elements of Semiology*. New York: Hill and Wang.

Radcliffe-Brown, A. R. 1952. *Structure and Function in Primitive Society*. London: Cohen and West.

Service, E. R. 1962. *Social Organization: An Evolutionary Perspective*. New York: Random House.

2 | The Individual in Society

In this chapter I want to try to find the basiç units of society before I go on to discuss human social groups. Two points will be made. First, the "individual" is a cultural category (particularly in American and Western culture) that is not very useful in understanding how most of the traditional world thinks and acts. Second, the reality we live in, the world that we take for granted, is something that we construct *socially*. It is as though we all engage in some giant conspiracy to nail down reality to a level that we can all understand and live in as well as live with, and that we do it together, that is, the act of "nailing down reality" is a social or collective act. The anthropologist works in exotic cultures where he or she can take very little for granted and can only begin to understand the society and the world of the traditional peoples by using the local logic. And by and large, the local logic of the people we study denies the primary importance of the individual and clearly shows that the world, or reality, is socially constructed.

THE "MYTH" OF THE INDIVIDUAL

When I was a beginning graduate student I had the privilege of sitting in on a discussion between an eminent psycholo-gist (Nevitt Sanford, the discoverer of the "authoritarian personality") and an equally eminent anthropologist (Gregory Bateson, who at that time was finishing his important work on the social basis of schizophrenia). I don't remember the topic of the conversation very well, but I do remember one dramatic pause which occurred during a discussion of the individual. "And what," said Bateson, "is the individual?" At the time I thought the remark was profoundly obtuse, because every schoolboy knows that the individual is a functioning organism that ends at the epidermis, is autonomous, endowed with free will, a capacity for good and for evil, a capacity for planning and locomotion, freedom, lust, creativity, genius and even boring conversation. But a moment's reflection will indicate that the "individual" is an idea that *we* have created over centuries of Western history; it is a cultural category, and as arbitrary as our distinction between "trees" and "bushes," "blue" and "green," "tree beetles" and "ground beetles," and so on. I am not saying that Westerners are deluded in seeing separate people "out there" and that the traditional world sees society or mankind as some kind of giant throbbing biomass. Rather, I am saying that most traditional societies do not make much of the cultural category of "the individual"; they see social reality as *social*, and not to be understood as aggregations of individuals. Let me borrow an example from the philosopher of science, Karl Popper. Imagine that you were trying to understand the direction of flight of a large cloud of locusts. One way you might try to observe the phenomenon is to observe the motion of each and every locust and try to figure out the movement of the cloud as the vectorial product of the flight path of each insect. Or, you could stand further back, forget about the individual, and observe the direction and velocity of the cloud as a whole. The first would land you up in what mathematicians call a "bushy mess": that is, computational problems of such difficulty that a solution would be almost impossible, whereas the second strategy would be quite simple and straightforward and would give you advance information on what wheat field needed protection. I think that most traditional societies design their social theories (and they *have* social theories, even though they lack advanced degrees in social science) with the social group as the central focus, not the individual.

ARE THERE TRULY INDIVIDUALISTIC SOCIETIES?

Human beings are social animals. But, we can certainly ask whether there are situations that affect individuals or whole societies where the individuals come to the forefront, and society is relegated to unimportance. This is a hard question to tackle since we rarely observe human beings out of society. It is rather like trying to discuss the hypothetical structure and form of a school of fish on dry land.

Periodically, however, "wolf children" are discovered. These are children who have either been orphaned, disowned, or have been locked in a room away from all human contact. When discovered, they are not quite human; that is, their behavior

is unworldly because it is not social behavior and, in cases of true isolation, (as in one case when a child was brought up in isolation by a deaf-mute mother) they lack language. Still they have the capacity for culture, and, in no case that I know of has a discovered "wolf child" not been able to acquire culture, sociability, and the capacity to share in social behavior, contracts, and communication to some degree.

EVERY MAN FOR HIMSELF IN A CONCENTRATION CAMP

But what about extreme conditions where one's life is at stake, and common sense would indicate that every person should look to themselves for their own salvation? Bruno Bettelheim, a psychoanalyst, was in a Nazi concentration camp during the early stages of World War II and was put under extreme stress and peril of his life, as were his fellow prisoners. Every effort was made to degrade the prisoners, to strip them of their personality, to make them into robots, and to tear apart any social fabric that might serve as the basis for a concerted attempt at resistance. The prisoners who attempted to maintain their "individuality," as (former) middle-class bankers or lawyers with ties to their families, friends, and past on the outside, tended not to survive. Those who adopted the new society, the new culture, and made it their own, and who joined the society of the prison camp even to the point of imitating the Gestapo guards, dressing like them and going to great pains to redesign their prison clothes to resemble the guards, tended to survive. In short, those who adapted to extreme cultural conditions and reformed their culture in accord with it had a more efficient survival technique than those who clung to the myth of the individual.

The literature on disasters indicates the

same thing: that as soon as the confusion and unreality right after the disaster passes, there is a strong, almost utopian, sense of sociability among disaster victims. Researchers talk about the creation of a "new social contract" in the aftermath of a disaster that belies the "war of all against all" picture of the man with the gun in his fallout shelter warding off his neighbors. This was a familiar topic of speculation during the early sixties when some felt we were at the brink of a nuclear war.

A recent book by Colin Turnbull (*The Mountain People*) can give us pause, however. The Ik, whom Turnbull studied for two years, came as close as any recorded people to reaching the stage of extreme individualism and the war of all against all. He presents us a picture of people who have recently been forbidden to practice their traditional ways and have been placed on a reservation where they are likely to starve to death. Here, he did find *individuals,* and the picture is neither pretty nor one we would endorse. People snatch food from the mouths of the sick and dying. A sick child is locked inside a hut and abandoned to die so that its complaints would not be heard by its family. A grandfather is joyfully beaten to death by his own grandchildren when he tries to protect some food and tobacco that Turnbull had given him. Turnbull continues:

Then the children began openly ridiculing him and teasing him, dancing in front of him and kneeling down so that he would trip over them. His grandson, who like all Ik children could lawfully joke with and tease his grandparents, stretched his teasing into playful beating, and used to creep up behind Lolim and with a pair of hard sticks drum a lively tatoo on the old man's bald head. Once Lolim, trying to cover his poor head with his bony arms, accidentally caught Arawa in the mouth. Instantly Arawa, with the back of his right hand, slapped Lolim as hard as he could on the side of his face, knocking the old man to the ground.

There were shrieks of delighted laughter, but as the old man lay still, not moving and not even crying, the fun wore thin, and when I approached, anthropological detachment long since departed, they had lost interest and went away.[1]

The case of the Ik stands alone in the ethnographic record, and, like many social scientists, I am not sure what to make of it. Perhaps the best thing to say is to claim that it is the rule-proving exception to my claim that man is a social animal.

WHEN IS A CRIME REALLY A CRIME?

In British and American jurisprudence a person who is insane at the time of the commission of a crime cannot be judged guilty. The rules for determining insanity were codified in England in 1843 and are referred to as the M'Naughten Rules. Though psychiatrists and jurists may differ on what constitutes insanity, the fact remains that in most jurisdictions, if a person cannot know the difference between right and wrong at the time of the commission of a crime he cannot be sentenced to prison, but must be put under psychiatric treatment.[2] This rule has saved first degree murderers from the death penalty, even though its importance today is much less than it was when the death penalty was given more freely.

But what about *sociological* M'Naughten Rules? In Victor Hugo's novel, *Les Misérables,* the main character, Jean Valjean, is a desperately poor man who steals

1. Colin Turnbull, *The Mountain People* (New York: Simon and Schuster, 1972).
2. Those of you who saw the film "Titticut Follies" or who have visited institutions for the criminally insane may find the difference between the treatment of insane offenders and general offenders consists more in the medication they receive than the conditions of detention, but that is not my point here.

a loaf of bread to feed his starving family and is hounded to death by society. But did he commit a crime? Under M'Naughten rules he did: he knew the difference between right and wrong. But obviously the novelist felt differently and pointed out a dilemma that runs deep in our society. Because we believe that moral responsibility resides in the *individual,* and that the *individual* is the important social unit of analysis in our theory of the social order we find ourselves in these dilemmas. We hang Adolf Eichmann for his crimes of genocide against the Jews because he is a responsible, moral person and we formulate the Nuremberg doctrine that the individual is morally responsible not to carry out an immoral order of a superior officer.

But not all societies see crime and criminality in this way. The Zapotec, whose ideas of crime and deviance I studied for seven years and recently reported in my book *Zapotec Deviance,* believe that the social order should be preserved just as we do, but they also see that crime and criminality reside in dislocations of the social order. They ignore the role of the individual. For example, they have a word and an idea that corresponds to our idea of "psychotic" or "crazy" but they don't even consider it to be a form of deviance. Deviance is a social dislocation, and crazy people, those who have lost their souls to a familiar spirit or have been bewitched, do not dislocate the social order or undermine the rules that order social intercourse. They do have a word for, and idea of, something that has the same feeling of seriousness with which we regard psychosis. I call it "abnormality." Abnormality is defined as occurring when a person is enmeshed in rotten social relations, particularly kinship relations. I state in the book:

Contrast . . . an American and a Zapotec trying to explain why they regard some person as ab-

normal. The American will dwell upon inferences about his psychological dispositions and could well summarize his statements by saying something like "he isn't all there," or "he is very neurotic," or "he has a screw loose." Even a word like *together* which in formal speech refers to social relations recently has taken on psychological significance, as in the statement "he's very together." The Zapotec would say, "his kinship relations are defective." He would not mean that he has a bad attitude toward his kinsmen, although that might be true; he means that the person is in an abnormal position because the matrix of relationships in which he is embedded is abnormal.[3]

In the same vein, it is interesting to contrast the Zapotec idea of rehabilitation with our own. I recently interviewed a group of prisoners in a Pennsylvania State Correctional Institute, and, in the style of an anthropologist, asked them about this "rehabilitation-stuff." I asked whether they knew anyone who had been rehabilitated in prison. They thought for a while and came up with some examples of people who had gone through conversion experiences, and, instead of doing what normal inmates do, they "caught religion" and started working like sweatshop operatives in the tailor's shop or peeled potatoes in the kitchen as though the world were going to end if every potato in the world wasn't peeled by tomorrow afternoon. (I am echoing their attitudes towards rehabilitation.) The prison residents obviously thought that a truly rehabilitated person was a real deviant. Recidivism rates further illustrate this viewpoint.[4]

In the Zapotec community where I studied there were two murderers when I

3. Henry A. Selby, *Zapotec Deviance* (Austin: University of Texas Press, 1974), p. 15.

4. The recidivism rate is the rate at which criminals return to prison. It varies from crime to crime, being low for murder and extremely high for forgery and burglary. Overall it is quite clear that what we mean by "rehabilitation" does not happen in prisons.

started my work in 1965, but by 1972 there were none. Both men were still in the community and both held responsible political and social offices. What they had both done, after a brief stay in prison and payment of a large fine, was to reactivate their kinship networks, and, in particular, the network that extends outward through godparents and godchildren. It took them five to six years to do it, but once they had established normal relationships within the village, a community-wide collective amnesia set in, since (by Zapotec logic) a person cannot be a serious deviant and good kin. Since the so-called murderers are good kin, they could not have been murderers. They had been "rehabilitated" because there are social mechanisms for re-integration into the community, and the social order takes precedence over the individual in the local logic.

DO WE SUBCONSCIOUSLY THINK LIKE THE ZAPOTECS?

No cultural system of ideas and symbols is free of paradox, and I have been overemphasizing our Western way of thinking of the individual as being the central idea in understanding behavior. We are no less intelligent than the Zapotecs and it is interesting to look at some new work in social psychology that shows that we aren't as thorough-going in our individualism as we might think.

Here is a true story and a common one that most of you will recognize! A graduate student and I were both working on papers last year which happened to have deadlines that coincided. Though we were both working fairly hard, it became clear that we were both going to be late in handing them in. When I found out that his was going to be late I became irritable and told him straight that I thought he would have to stop being inefficient, lazy, and irresponsible if he wanted to succeed in

graduate school. He was a friend so he could come right back at me and ask me about my paper. "Well," I said, "that's completely different. I have had to look after my kids because my wife is working, my mother-in-law has been visiting, I am on all these damn committees in the University, and I simply don't have the time!" There was a broad smile from the graduate assistant who recognized rationalization when he heard it. But the fact of the matter is that we all think this way. We ourselves (we say to ourselves) would be good, upright, and virtuous if it were not for the circumstances that force us to be otherwise. Our behavior is sociologically and culturally constrained, to use the vocabulary of chapter 1. Other people's behavior can be attributed to their personality or character. There are a number of results in social psychology that bear out this general tendency we have to see ourselves in a sociological manner and others as "bloody-minded." The proper name for the subject is "attribution theory" since it studies the way people go about attributing causes to other peoples' behavior. So it seems fair to conclude that we are at least partially aware of the role that others play in shaping our conduct—just like the Zapotecs.

Why is this tendency to individualism and individualistic thinking to be found in Western societies? We can only speculate. My own view is that it has nothing to do with the value we place on human life, or on the individual, or anything like that. Societies vary in this regard and we would be foolhardy to think that we place any greater value of life, or loathe human suffering any more than anyone else. It most likely stems from the fact that our society is a mobile, fractionated, complex society, and not at all small-scale or homogeneous like small communities in traditional society. We see people whom we do not know well in such a variety of roles and in such a transitory fashion that we have to make quick decisions about them. We are aware of the uniqueness of each person's biography, and when we catch up on other people's news, it is to find out about their unique experiences. We don't see them in stable social roles, and in particular, the same social roles that we ourselves occupy, just as our parents did. Gearing has expressed the same feelings about the Fox Indians as I have about the Zapotec, and summarizes his view as follows:

Our contemporary Western life draws into sharpest focus the birth and continuing flow of experience and the resulting personal qualities of mind of individual human organisms; when we meet another we want to know where he has been, what he has done, what kind of man he has become and where he seems to be going. As for that other dimension of reality, enduring organization, [what I have been calling the sociological matrix] we of course must continually act in its terms and are therefore aware of it at some level of mental activity. We think often, for example, of those aspects of organization that affect and express ranked status. But it seems that we rarely think about enduring organization with clarity and direction and completeness, except under special circumstances (as when we are required to describe the table of organization of a factory.) To appear to think consistently in everyday life about one's social positions and the positions of one's fellows seems, to us, a little indecent.

For the Fox, the emphasis appears to be reversed. The primary reality habitually considered with full awareness by a Fox, somewhat systematically and with clarity and direction is enduring organization. A Fox...sees another most concretely and precisely when he views him as an incumbent in a social slot, sees himself moving into the slot, occupying it at the moment and acting appropriately or now, and moving out. Primary Fox reality is, I believe, such a system of special positions that endure. I think of my friend: "Joe (who is a father) . . . ."
A Fox thinks of his friend: "This father (who is Joe) . . . ."[5]

THE SOCIAL CONSTRUCTION OF REALITY

One final point will conclude this discussion of the unimportance of the idea of the individual in understanding human social organization. Not only are we social animals, but the world we live in is a social invention: reality is constructed by people getting together and acting collectively so as to agree upon what they can take for granted.

The philosopher Bradley, a hard-nosed commonsensical Britisher, was once heard to comment on the more esoteric forms of German metaphysics in the following way: "If any man tells me that I cannot know whether breakfast comes before lunch, and lunch before dinner, then I will have to inform him that he is a damn fool!" The sociologist Garfinkel, a Californian, once instructed his students to go home and without telling anyone, to act as though they were guests in their own houses, with their own families. When the students returned two days later the experiment had to be called off, because of the near-riots that they had produced, particularly at the dinner table. Both these examples emphasize that there is a real reality "out there" which can be taken for granted (lunch comes before dinner) and that if one acts to confound the taken-for-granted assumptions about that reality, one is liable to start a near-riot.

Because that reality is so "solid," so palpable, and so real we *can* take it for granted, just as we take walking for granted until we stumble and breathing until we choke. And just because that real reality is so important *and* taken-for-granted, we have to study it, and see what form it takes (thus Garfinkel's experiment which was designed to find out what kind of thing was taken-for-granted in family discourse).

5. Fred Gearing, *The Face of the Fox* (Chicago: Aldine, 1970), pp. 137-38.

Reality (and culture) existed before we did in a coherent form that we learned. We took in reality's assumptions like mother's milk, and the assumptions are deep within us. The assumptions are coded in language, often, and since we often communicate with the use of language, they are assumptions that we share in order to communicate. "Common sense" or what the historian called the stock of knowledge that "every schoolboy knows" is an important part of that real reality; without our sharing it with others we would not be able to communicate with them (nor form a social and cultural, i.e., human unit.)

We live in *multiple* realities and can separate them out readily. We don't confuse what we dream with what we experience in our conscious lives nor do we confuse a hallucination with everyday consciousness. In fact, we endow consciousness with a special significance and regard it as representing reality. Reality occurs in the "here and now," and occurs in *time*. Time has a special meaning for us because it locates us and ensures that we know we are sane. Psychotics lose time; alcoholics who have blackouts lose days or weeks of time; amnesiacs lose parts of their lives. They all find that when they lose time, they become very anxious.

Two more points: first, social facts, activities, and events are *things*. They have a reality that is thing-like. When we know something "really happened," we endow it with the properties of an *object*, or in fancier terms, it becomes an *objectification*. And these objectifications are coded in language, communicated to others, and *negotiated*.

Let me give an example of negotiation. Eleanor Maccoby, a social psychologist, used to perform the following experiment with her introductory classes. Without warning the door to the classroom would burst open and a young man being pursued by another would rush into the room, run around the lectern, and hurry out the door. As soon as the door slammed behind the pair, she would ask, "What on earth happened?" The students would respond with a variety of different versions: some would say that the pursuer had a knife in his hand, another would say it was a kind of fraternity prank (an older version of "streaking"), and the discussion would proceed until a reality had been *negotiated* between the various versions.

When there is sufficient conformity, or agreement, about the nature and form of certain happenings (and meanings), then we can talk about an *institution*. An institution is a set of ideas that is socially negotiated and agreed upon, usually in language, given a name, objectified, and thereby takes on the trappings of reality and becomes a part of our conscious world.

They are objects that we encounter in everyday life: the family, the religious order, the natural world, meal times, are *instituted*. Children are wonderful informants about institutions and their objective quality. "How can we have lunch if we haven't had breakfast?" my nephew asked me last Sunday, since he hadn't learned the meaning of the cultural category "brunch."

But I don't have to go on about this. Anthropologists are students of everyday life in a variety of different contexts. Everyday life is *socially constituted* and seen as having an objective reality that is "really real."

Anthropologists report, generally, the outcome of the negotiations, as when they say, "In Zapotec witches murder people, kill animals, and do all manner of bodily harm." The Zapotec agree to this, and therefore witches have an objective reality to them that is lacking for us, since we neither believe in "witches," nor agree with the Zapotec about what is real. Reality changes from culture to culture, because, in part, social conditions change from culture to culture. But always, reality is a giant network of agreements about what is real and factual and the product of social interaction.

In a word, not only can we not exist as human beings in isolation, as individuals, there cannot even be a reality "out there" without society, without interaction, argument, and (in a phrase that will recur throughout) the exchange of symbols.

For Further Reading

Berger, Peter, and Thomas Luckman (1967) *The Social Construction of Reality*. New York. Anchor Books. Even though you will find this book hard going at first, it is the best introduction to the phenomenological view of reality in print.

Ornstein, Robert (1972) *The Psychology of Consciousness*. San Francisco. Freeman. This is a fascinating book about new developments in psychology that have overturned our traditional ideas about what consciousness is. It explores the relationships between esoteric "mystic" traditions. such as Yoga and Sufi, and modern psychological analysis.

Selby, H. A. (1974) *Zapotec Deviance: The Convergence of Folk and Modern Sociology*. Austin. University of Texas Press. This is a full account of how the author came to understand that the view of the "individual" was a Western myth. A study of crime and deviance in a traditional, Mesoamerican, Indian community.

Turnbull, Colin (1972) *The Mountain People*. New York. Simon and Schuster. This is one of the most surprising and disturbing ethnographies of recent times.

Bibliography

Berger, Peter and Luckman, Thomas 1967. *The Social Construction of Reality*. New York: Anchor Books.

Gearing, Fred 1970. *The Face of the Fox*. Chicago: Aldine.

Selby, H. A. 1974. *Zapotec Deviance: The Convergence of Folk and Modern Sociology*. Austin: University of Texas Press.

3 | Social Organization: The Logical Beginnings

INTRODUCTION

In this chapter we will examine the logical beginnings, the underpinnings of human social organization. I will first discuss the difference between society and culture, then social units, and cultural units. Next we will look at what many anthropologists believe to be the essential ingredient without which human social organization as we know it could not exist, that is, the *incest taboo*. I am going to try to persuade you that it is the incest taboo that creates the basic distinction upon which all organization is based: the *me/you* distinction, or, the *my group/other group* distinction.

SOCIETY AND CULTURE

First some definitions. What is society? Very simply, it is the arrangement of warm bodies in space and time. What are *social units*? They are sometimes aggregations and sometimes groups of warm bodies that make up an organization larger than themselves. The warm bodies are an aggregation if they are an accidental gathering without any particular structure. A crowd at a football game is an aggregation. A swarm of moths circling a light bulb is also an aggregation. A *group* has structure. An aggregation can turn into a group as, for example, when an aggregation of milling

people turns into a lynch mob. As soon as a leader emerges and a set of ideas is transferred from one member to another, and the element of *purpose* is introduced into the behavior of the aggregation, it becomes a group.

We contrast society and social units with *culture* and *cultural units*. Culture is a set of ideas that is learned, patterned, and transmitted from generation to generation. Cultural units are ideas which are often coded in language and provide us with the raw material of cultural systems. A cultural unit is any category of events which we choose to recognize. Railroad trains, beauty, hippy, pine tree, autonomic nervous system, and poetry are all cultural units, fortunately coded in language, since if they were not I couldn't write them down. When the cultural units are coded in language, we call them *conscious cultural categories*. When they are not, we call them *unconscious* cultural categories. Unconscious cultural categories are often "differences that make a difference," to borrow a brilliant and powerful phrase from Gregory Bateson. For example, Berlin, Breedlove, and Raven found out that Tzeltal Indians sort kinds of corn into different groupings because they know there is a difference that makes a difference, although they do not have any name for the two groupings. Prison guards recognize a whole series of differences that make a difference between kinds of prisoners (or "residents"), but they cannot tell you what they are since they don't have names for them. They say (and the Tzeltal Indian would echo their thoughts most likely) that they have a "gut feeling" or a "seat of the pants feeling" about certain kinds of prisoners that tells them either not to hassle them or, on the contrary, to give them a "write up" for similar bad conduct. Judges and policemen report the same; particularly the police when they have to decide whether or not to make an arrest. All of these unconscious categories are cultural units.

WHAT THEN IS UNIQUE ABOUT HUMAN SOCIETY?

I will make the flat claim that the unique feature of our society that distinguishes it from any other society is the *incest taboo*, that is, the existence of a rule (or if we are talking about animals, a stable behavior) that creates two classes of opposite sex fellow species members: those with whom the animal may have sexual relations and, more importantly, those with which the animal may not.

The incest taboo is universal in human society. It takes a variety of forms, but there is a universal human rule against sexual relations within the nuclear family (i.e. the elementary family composed of father, mother, and children). Nuclear incest is morally tabooed everywhere. But although there are examples of societies where the rule against sexual relations extends to whole communities or large classes of relatives, it is also true that there is always an example, somewhere, of a society where sexual relations with any close relative are permitted. It may be the mother-in-law, a first cousin, a wife's sister, or an aunt with whom sexual relations are permitted or even encouraged, but the taboo on nuclear incest is universal.

WHY IS THE TABOO ON NUCLEAR INCEST UNIVERSAL?

The question as to why the prohibition on sexual relations between mother and son, father and daughter, and brother and sister is provocative, and has elicited a flood of comment and theorizing. Two psychological explanations are often given and they are diametrically opposed. The first explanation, which was Sigmund Freud's, says that the reason we have an incest taboo is to prevent boys' fulfilling the deep-seated instinctual sexual urge to copulate with our mothers, and secondarily with our sisters in place of our mothers. Much of Freud's theory was male dominated, and his theory of maturation and the acquisition of a mature adult identity was linked to his views on mother-son incest. In his view, if the young boy is to arrive at a mature genital sexuality which includes the ability to form proper *object relations* (i.e. mature sexual relations with women outside his immediate family), he must somehow divest himself of his female identity acquired from his close relationship with his mother as an infant and young child and identify with the father. At first the child wants to dispose of the father and replace him. But when the realization dawns that he cannot do this, he gets around it by identifying with the father, and thereby possessing the mother through the father, and establishing male identity. The conflict that he experiences during this period is called *Oedipal conflict*, after Oedipus, prince of Thebes, who unknowingly murdered his father and married his mother.

Freud's reasoning seems sound in broad outline, if not in detail. Clinical evidence from psychology has pretty well vindicated the existence of Oedipal conflict in Western society, although cross-cultural work indicates it has more to do with people's feelings about authority than with their sexuality.

An opposing view, which was stated by Westermarck in his book, *The History of Human Marriage*, says that the incest taboo simply codifies the universal human feeling of uninterest, or lack of sexual arousal toward members of the opposite sex with whom we are very familiar.[1] There is some interesting evidence for this conclusion, drawn from experimental psychology and anthropology. Leslie Segner, an experimental psychologist with interests in anthropology, carried out an experiment where she measured the level of sexual arousal among laboratory rats. She found that "distance lent enhancement." Rats that were both cage mates from birth and brother-sister pairs (siblings) showed less sexual arousal than rats who were cage mates from birth but not siblings, and they in turn showed less interest than rats who were placed in the same cage close to the time of sexual maturity.[2]

Some evidence that supports Westermarck's position was gathered by Arthur Wolf, an anthropologist who studied in Taiwan, where the practice of arranged marriage persists in some families. When parents arrange marriages, the girl is brought to live in the husband's house when they are both very young, and they grow up like brother and sister. He found that sexual relations were less satisfactory in these marriages, as compared to marriages between people who were not childhood associates, as measured by the higher frequency with which men sought sex from prostitutes, higher frequency of adultery among wives, higher divorce rates, and lower rates of sexual intercourse.[3]

The psychological evidence for the existence of the incest taboo is conflicting. The *sociological* evidence is also hard to evaluate. Malinowski made the sensible claim that if nuclear incest were permitted in the elementary family, then sexual jealousy would tear the fabric of the family apart. The authority of the older generation which was necessary for the transmission and preservation of the culture over time would be destroyed, and societies that practiced nuclear incest would wipe themselves out.[4] But the evidence is difficult and fragmentary. Now that people feel freer to report on their sexual behavior than they did in Malinowski's time, or even at the time of the Kinsey report, more cases of "normal" incest are coming to light. A recent report in New York Magazine (hardly a scientific source, but scientific reports are hard to come by) indicated that brother-sister incest might be much more common than usually supposed, and examples were given of very close, sexual relations between brother and sister were carried on to the mutual satisfaction of the participants until such time as they "grew out of it," that is, went off to college, or found greater sexual satisfaction with partners outside the nuclear family. The case of father/daughter incest is less clear. In those few (eleven) cases studied by Kaufman, Peck and Tagiuri, the family seemed very disorganized before the occurrence of incest, and in every case that was closely studied, the mother participated in arranging the relationship, or condoned it by completely withdrawing. Very little is known about mother/son in-

1. E. Westermarck, *The History of Human Marriage* (London: Macmillan & Co., 1922).
2. Her measure of sexual arousal was "latency to copulation," which is the time that elapses before first copulation.
3. Arthur Wolf, "Childhood Association, Sexual Attraction and the Incest Taboo: A Chinese Case," *American Anthropologist* 68(1966): 883-98.
4. Bronislaw Malinowski, *Sex and Repression in Savage Society* (Boston: Beacon Press, 1924).

cest and perhaps for that reason it is assumed to be much less frequent.[5]

The biogenetic argument is clearest. It seems quite clear, despite the counter claims of some animal breeders, that hybridization or outbreeding is selectively advantageous in all breeding populations. One way we can account for the origin of the incest taboo is to assume that Paleolithic man was as intelligent as we are and was able to observe the comparative disadvantages of inbreeding. Segner and Collins noted that roughly one-third of the myths involving incest recounted physical defects or sterility as a direct result.[6] Much of the data on the deleterious genetic effects of incestuous unions has been collated by Lindzey. It has been calculated that if inbreeding continued in a population for twenty generations, then each member of the population would be genetically identical to every other, and therefore the adaptability of the population would be very low: if a change took place in the environmental conditions, the breeding population would have no resilience. Certainly, the occurrence of lethal genes in inbred populations is higher than in outbreeding populations. Lindzey cites Adams and Neel's data[7] on a comparison between eighteen children of incestuous matings and eighteen children from homes and families that were the same without the incest. He states:

Adams and Neel (1957)...compared the children of 18 nuclear incest matings (12 brother-sister, and 6 father-daughter) with 18 control matings, rather closely matched with the incest group for age, weight, stature, intelligence and socioeconomic status. At the end of 6 months they found that of the 18 children of an incestuous union, five had died; two were severely mentally retarded, were subject to seizures and had to be institutionalized; one had a bilateral cleft palate; and three showed evidence of borderline intelligence (estimated IQ 70). Thus, only 7 of the 18 children were considered free of pathology and ready for adoption. On the other hand, none of the 18 control children had died or were institutionalized, none was severely mentally retarded, and 15 were considered ready for adoption.[8]

Now the problem with data such as this is that it surely looks like plausible proof of the assertion that nuclear incest is so obviously deleterious that cultured humans could hardly overlook it. But we cannot know whether the abnormalities of the children of the incestuous matings occurred because of genetic defects, or from the *fact* that they were specially treated. Their parents were *deviants*, the children were abnormal as society defines abnormal, and we know just enough about the relationship between people's feelings about themselves and illness (i.e. psychosomatic pathology) to know that we cannot disentangle the knot entirely. But if the effects are as dramatic as they appear to be, it does not seem likely to have escaped the notice of a culture-bearing human.

Whatever caused the incest taboo, there is one immediate result: the formation of alliances. If I cannot marry my sister but

5. Irving Kaufman, Alice C. Peck, and Consuelo K. Tagiuri, "The Family Constellation and Overt Incestuous Relations between Father and Daughter," *American Journal of Orthopsychiatry* 24 (1954): 266-71.

6. Leslie Segner and A. Collins, "A Cross Cultural Study of Incest Myths." (manuscript, Austin: University of Texas, 1967).

7. Adams, S. and J. V. Neel, "Children of Incest," *Pediatrics* 40 (1957): 55-62.

8. Gardner Lindzey, "Some Remarks Concerning Incest, the Incest Taboo and Psychoanalytic Theory," *American Psychologist* 22 (1967): 1054.

must marry yours then I have to create a system of social classification that distinguishes my group from your group, and the idea that we *exchange* women (or men, it doesn't matter) means that we are allied. Once the incest taboo is established then it has a positive selective advantage that is not only genetic but also sociological, political, and evolutionary. Wolves are successful in the hunt because they can cooperate. Culture-bearing human beings are successful in the hunt because they can not only cooperate and communicate, but they can call upon the ties they have with those with whom they exchange spouses, and thereby create a web of alliances that would give them a selective advantage (other things being equal) over groups that did not have this custom.

In short, the incest taboo, like other deeply seated and defining characteristics of humanity, is *overdetermined* (i.e. it has many causes) and *multifinal* (that is, has many outcomes). And in the end the important thing is not to account for the origin of the incest taboo, but to examine its consequences so that we can come to understand the basis of human society.

Bibliography

Adams, S., and J. V. Neel. 1957. "Children of Incest," *Pediatrics* 40:55-62.

Lévi-Strauss, Claude 1969. *The Elementary Structures of Kinship*. Boston: Beacon Press.

Malinowski, B. 1929. *The Sexual Life of Savages in Northwestern Melanesia*. London: Routledge and Kegan Paul.

Schneider, D. M. 1968. *American Kinship: A Cultural Account*. Englewood Cliffs: Prentice-Hall.

4 | The Family

INTRODUCTION

The smallest world that can exist is a two-person world: the elementary social unit is the *dyad* (interacting group of two persons). The elementary unit of social analysis is the *relation* between two people. Social analysis deals with relations and not with the elements of the relation, just as physics deals with the relationships between elements which together form a structure of relations.

The most elementary form of complex dyadic relations, in turn, is *the family* which, in one form or another, is almost universal. The family is a set of relations; the *nuclear family* consists of six such relations: father-son, father-daughter, mother-son, mother-daughter, husband-wife, and brother-sister. We call these elementary relationships *primary,* and we abbreviate them in the language of kinship as F, M, B, Z, S, D, H, W to indicate "father," "mother," "brother," "sister," "son," "daughter," "husband," and "wife." And we diagram the relationships in a genealogical plate as follows:

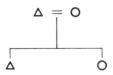

$\Delta \doteq$ "male"

$O \doteq$ "female"

$| \doteq$ "ascending link"

$— \doteq$ "sibling link"

$= \doteq$ "marriage link"

and $\doteq$ means "is defined as"

We used to think that the nuclear family was universal, in part because we knew that kinship relations were universal. No known society lacks a kinship system, not even the Ik who treat each other so abominably in our view. And kinship systems are made up of kinfolk, and kinfolk are related to us in *genealogical* ways. And genealogy is a way of analyzing our kinship relations by using the relationships of the nuclear family. For example if I want to list all those relationships that qualify for the *kin term* "uncle" in my dialect of American English, I can write them out very simply as "Uncle" = {FB ∪ MB ∪ FZH ∪ MZH}, which is a short way of saying that my uncle is one or all of the following sets of relations: "father's brother," "mother's brother," "father's sister's husband," and "mother's sister's husband."

But although our logic may have seemed impeccable, it doesn't hold up under extensive ethnographic examination. It is cer-

19

tainly true that every society has a kinship system, and it is also true that we can analyze kinship relations genealogically. It is also true that our system of genealogical reckoning is based upon the eight primary relations that define the nuclear family, and it would seem logical to suppose that the Paleolithic peoples didn't pick these out of thin air, but based their system of reckoning on primary relationships, and maybe, if we could interview them they would agree to these propositions. But so far as contemporary peoples are concerned, there are too many exceptions to the proposition to allow us to state categorically that the nuclear family is universal.

The best known exception is the Nayar people, a warrior subcaste of Malabar, India, who live in what Americans would call "absent-father" households. Kathleen Gough had to reconstruct their ethnography, but it seems pretty clear that the family was made up of a woman and her children. In place of a "father," there was the mother's brother. The "father" was an elusive figure. A young Nayar girl was married after she reached menarche, but she didn't live with her husband, nor did he come to live with her. He might have sexual relations with her on their bridal night, but then again he might not. But his brothers, and fellow clan members of his generation would have rights of sexual access to her, and confusion over who was sleeping with the "wife" was obviated by the ruse of leaving a spear outside the door of the hut in order to indicate "occupied." And the "wife" was permitted to take on lovers, while the men of her group were equally free to roam as visiting husbands, or passing lovers in other clan groups.[1]

Beside the Nayar, there are numerous cases of *matrifocal* households found throughout Latin America and parts of Africa, where the family unit is made up of a mother and her children, so it seems pretty safe to conclude that the nuclear family is not universal.

IS KINSHIP BIOLOGICAL OR SOCIOLOGICAL, AND WHO CARES?

When we use terms like "father" or "mother," and define uncle as "father's brother," "mother's brother," and so on, it sounds like we are talking about bilogical relations. We have a cultural belief, for example, that both the mother and the father contribute some "biogenetic material" to their offspring.[2] We base this premise on routine statements that Americans make about kinship relations. Americans say things like, "Imagine if she has her father's looks and her mother's brains!", which are supposed to be funny, but which in turn can only be meaningful if we assume that both the father and the mother contribute. But, the fact of the matter is that kinship is sociological in nature.

Take the term "father." It is a kin term in American English. It implies that the male in question transmitted the genetic materials to the child through a woman, usually the "mother" (in our culture). But what if the mother was rather loose in her association before or during the marriage. Can we be sure that the mother's husband is indeed the "father" of the child in question? Obviously not. Paternity laws exist, but paternity is very hard to prove or disprove. That is why in Roman law it was quite clear: "the father is the mother's husband." And the practice is generally followed in our own society. All the folderol that at-

1. Kathleen Gough, "The Nayars and the Definition of Marriage," *Journal of the Royal Anthropological Institute* 89 (1959): 23-24.

2. The term is from David M. Schneider, *American Kinship: A Cultural Account* (Englewood Cliffs, N.J.: Prentice-Hall, 1968).

tends the trauma of telling a child that he or she was adopted derives from our notion that it is somehow unnatural to be brought up by people whom one regards as mother and father, but with whom one does not share this biogenetic substance. For the sake of analysis, we can distinguish between the *social father* (or *pater*), and the *genetic father*, who was the man whose identity may be known only to his confessor or psychiatrist, but who contributed the genes. Some societies go further. In some parts of Australia, for example, there is a role for the "firestick father," who is a person designated by the society as the one who contributed the spirit essence that gave birth to the child. In this case, we call the "firestick father" the *genitor*, i.e., the person who is socially recognized to have played a critical role in engendering the child. So, for the sake of analysis, there are three terms: *pater*, *genitor*, and *genetic father*. The first two are socially recognized, and the third may or may not be known. But the point is that for a biologically based theory of kinship, only the last would be important. And, in contrast, what we record on our kinship charts and genealogies is the *pater*, the socially defined father.

A little thought will indicate that the same ideas can be applied to the mother, yielding *mater*, *genetrix*, and *genetic mother*. If you think that the last two distinctions could never matter, you have not read your British history and seen the great lengths that royalty went to to ensure that a baby wasn't smuggled into the royal bedchamber in a bedpan, and that the queen was *genetrix* and *genetic mother* of the royal heir.

Royal bedpans are quaint, but some of the other consequences of our beliefs about the bases of kinship are not so quaint. We believe that the analytic categories of *pater*, *genitor*, and *genetic father* should all converge on one person (that is, they should be the same person). I have already mentioned the trauma of the moment when adopted parents reveal that their children are not quite "theirs," despite the clear fact that as parents they have played the only important social roles of parent to the children. Another consequence of our cultural belief is the belief in illegitimacy. How on earth, in a rational world, can a child be illegitimate? "Children are children" say the Zapotec, adding, "some of the town people talk about 'children of the street' meaning children whose mothers had sex with other men, but this is nonsense. Children need and always have the love of parents and kin: the father and mother will bring them up!" But with our cultural beliefs in the importance of biogenetic substances, we say things like, "genes will out," and thereby endow the child with a set of expectations about his or her behavior that can be at best confusing, and at worst profoundly destructive.

Some people respond to this questioning of the whole idea of legitimacy versus illegitimacy by citing the problem of inheritance. Somehow it is wrong that inheritance not follow the "bloodline," from which the "illegitimate child" is excluded. But what nonsense to equate the inheritance of genes with the inheritance of property. Rules of property-transfer across generations presumably exist to minimize debate and conflict over valuables, not to prop up some biological theory. One might just as well say that the chairmanship of the board of General Motors should pass down some bloodline, if the theory is that important and basic. Property can pass across generations in any number of ways: all of them sociologically defined. It can pass from mother's brother to sister's son (in a matrilineal society), or it can pass from father to father's younger brother (in some patrilineal societies), or it can revert to the state (as it partially does under our laws of taxation).

But the notion of illegitimacy is important, say others (including some of our policy makers) for the maintenance of the family, and the proper rearing of the children. Again, what nonsense! If children are reared alone without any male who is closely affiliated with them, it may be damaging, so much may be true. But to say that a "child born out of wedlock" is somehow deprived of the companionship of senior generation males is to assume that mother belongs to some kind of cloistered all female kin group, and, as we pointed out in the Nayar case, where the child never knows or sees his or her father, there are plenty of males around for him or her to relate to: all the males of mother's matrilineal group, for starters.

But the notion persists. There was a recent raging debate over a government report, the Moynihan Report, which indicated that the basis of the problems of black Americans lay in the rate of illegitimacy which was (in 1963) running at 23.6 percent for blacks as compared to 3.1 percent for whites.[3] As Jones and Ryan have pointed out, this may only mean that white society is so sick that it wants to rid itself of its most precious asset—its own children—through the use of abortion (then illegal), Enovid, or adoption, sentiments and mechanisms that are not precisely shared by the black community.[4] But the anthropologist wonders why the argument arose in the first place. First, how do we know that the symbol "father" means precisely the same in white and black culture? If cultures differ, and if the argument can be made that there is a black culture and a black kinship system which includes symbols such as "mother," "father," "son," and "daughter," who is to say without the appropriate culturally sensitive study, that the symbol "father" means the same in both. We would certainly not make the claim that "padre de familia" ("father of the family") means exactly the same to *chicanos*, or Latin Americans as "father" means to us. We know better than that!

But, the argument proceeds, we are not talking about symbols, or meanings, we are talking about absent fathers and broken families! Take the idea of "absent father": who is more absent—the black male who visits his children, sees them in the street, who recognizes them, and demands their respect, or the father whose family lives in the suburbs while he commutes to work and (in the cliché) drinks three martinis on his way home at night, arriving just in time to put the kids to bed, and fall into the television set? And what about broken families? Is it not just possible that the family is somewhat differently defined among lower-class blacks (for whom these studies are written), and is it not just possible that they wouldn't know they were living in broken families unless someone told them they were? It could well be the case that a "broken family" was a middle-class white idea, and perfectly appropriate for middle-class white culture. A divorce that leaves a woman with small children stranded in a house in the suburbs, in a society that lives in couples and denies social lives to singles, is different from a divorce or separation or even abandonment in a society where mothers with children are not seen to be impaired in any way, but, quite the contrary, as strong, normal, competent, and not deviant in the slightest.

3. Daniel P. Moynihan, *The Negro Family: the Case for National Action* (Washington, D.C.: United States Printing Office, 1965).

4. James Jones, *Prejudice and Racism* (Reading, Mass.: Addison-Wesley, 1972) and W. Ryan, "Savage Discovery: the Moynihan Report," in *The Moynihan Report and the Politics of Controversy*, ed. L. Rainwater and W. L. Yancey (Cambridge, Mass.: MIT Press, 1967).

HOW THE REST OF THE WORLD LIVES

Most of the world believes that outsiders, whether they be witches, or sorcerers, or enemies, or strangers, are the people who harm you, and make you sick. We believe quite the opposite. People who are far from us may be odious in all kinds of ways, but they are marginal to our existence. As Freud pointed out so clearly, and as our psychiatrists help us discover, in Western society it is the family that makes you sick. For boys, it is the unresolved Oedipal conflicts that seem to stand in the way of a fully mature life that leads to the Freudian ideal of being able to love and to work. For girls the identity problem is somewhat less complicated, but once again relationships of power and sexual identity within the family engender the deep conflicts that disrupt their later lives.

It must be no coincidence that families in the rest of the world differ, for the most part, from our *nuclear* model. First of all, the preponderance of societies in the world (54 percent in Textor's Cross Cultural Summary) live in *extended families,* that is, families in which there are at least three generations represented.[5] An even greater preponderance (79 percent) live in societies with plural marriage (almost always polygyny, or the practice that favors the marriage of a man with more than one wife). And even independent families, like our own, favor polygyny more than three to one over our *monogamous* (having one spouse) practice.

The single most frequent form of family organization is the *patrilineal extended family,* which consists of an older couple, their married *sons,* their married sons' children, and their own unmarried children. Less frequently found, but still more frequent than our nuclear family, is the *matrilineal extended family,* which is made up of an older couple, their married *daughters,* their married daughters' chil-

dren, and their own unmarried children. Extended families worldwide seem to be preferred by far and away the most societies.

Compared to the nuclear family, the extended family has its advantages and drawbacks. Its advantages can best be seen from the point of view of the child, whose aunts and uncles will be around (and usually given "parent-like" status by being called "mother" and "father"), as well as the grandparents with whom warm, close relationships are found worldwide. The child can turn to these people for support, love, comfort, and perhaps most important, help in understanding the parents. In our society it is a big step to go outside the nuclear family for such things.

But there are drawbacks, too. First of all you have to be able to get along with a lot of people. Privacy is at a minimum. Now, to be sure, people who are brought up in extended families don't have the same (exaggerated?) feelings about putting fences between them and their neighbors as we do. My children, for example, always found it unnatural to come home from the Zapotec village where we lived and go back to sleeping *alone,* after they had become used to sleeping five or six to a bed or sleeping mat in what they affectionately referred to as the "family pile." But, at the same time, and in the same village, I knew a young couple who had recently married and wished to have sexual relations frequently and did not like to have an audience accompanying them and were irritated by the fact that they had to go out to the corn fields to avoid the prying eyes of the community. As with most things, there is a trade-off between a sense of security and a sense of privacy.

And there can also be conflicts between

5. Robert Textor, *A Cross-Cultural Summary* (New York: Human Relations Area Press, 1967).

the generations. The Irish family was notable for such conflicts: the son "waiting around" for the old man to die so that he could inherit and become a man in his own right, and some social scientists feel that the heavy drinking and brawling of the Irish males arose from the frustrations involved. But sometimes the children don't have to wait around for the father to die: there are societies where there are rules that state that the rights and obligations of full manhood pass to the heir when the heir "comes of age," however that be defined. And that can bring trouble. In one African case (the people of the Nuba hills) there was a rule that the heir, in this case the sister's son, since the families were *matrilineal*, inherited before the elder was ready to give up the political, executive, and economic rights that he had previously owned (he didn't want to retire, because sometimes retirement was required before the age of thirty). Witchcraft accusations resulted, which are a symptom of tremendous hostility: each accusing the other directly or indirectly of trying to commit murder, the one to gain his rightful place, the other not to lose it.

Looking at family arrangements from the point of view of the individual, the choice between a nuclear family and an extended one depends on one's preference for privacy, independence, and mobility over security, dependence, and a sense of rootedness. I frankly think that the movement to communes, rap groups, and ethnic, social, and political groups is an attempt to rebuild the feeling of extended kinship in America, and that the use of the terms "brother" and "sister" among group members reflects that feeling of lost kinship. I do not believe that the independent nuclear family is a capitalist plot to destroy the fabric of society in order to make labor as mobile as possible, and dependent on employers and capital as possible. But it seems true that industrialization and urbanization break down extended family arrangements, and, if you believe, as I do, that kinship relationships are fundamental to the good life, *and* you are an optimist, you can take encouragement from the fact that worldwide extended family arrangements predominate, and that it is only in the recent past that these arrangements have broken down.

MARRIAGE AND THE FAMILY

By plural marriage we mean cultural practices that favor the marriage of a person of one sex to multiple spouses. When one man marries a number of women, we call the practice *polygyny*, and when one woman marries a number of men, we call the practice *polyandry*. Polygyny is very common; polyandry extremely rare. Marriage is impossible to define, really. A traditional definition taken from *Notes and Queries*, which is a how-to-do-it anthropological field manual that tells you what-it-is-when-you-are-looking-at-it, states that marriage is a "union between a man and a woman such that the children born to the woman are recognized legitimate offspring of both parents." Marriage is the institution that provides the child with a *mater* and a *pater*. But, more importantly, it is an *alliance* between two groups. Recall, if you will, the discussion of *incest*, the rule that forbids certain classes of people from having sexual intercourse. There is another rule, quite different from incest, found in every society, that defines the group from whom one can draw a spouse (husband or wife).[6] These are the

---

6. Robin Fox remarks in his book *Kinship and Marriage* (highly recommended reading!) that although every schoolboy could distinguish between sex and marriage, anthropologists seemed to have insuperable difficulties, judging by the fact that they constantly seem to confuse incest (which has to do with sexual relation) and endogamy/exogamy which have to do with marriage.

rules of *exogamy* and *endogamy*, and they vary widely from society to society. We are most sensitive to the rules of endogamy if not entirely consciously so. Every American parent can tell their child the kind of spouse that is suitable for the family. In England (among the middle and upper classes) they are explicit: "Are you sure he is of our class and background, my dear?" In America, except among certain ethnic groups, we are less explicit: "Are you sure he would make you happy, my dear; do you share enough interests and friends?" In both America and England exogamous rules are only invoked when one petitions to marry one's first cousin.

In a word, the endogamous rules state how extensive the "spouse pool" is. Exogamous rules state how close to the family you can get, and not break the rule. In traditional South India, for example, both were well defined: the rule of endogamy stated that you had to marry within your caste, or sometimes your subcaste. Brahmins do not marry Sweepers. The rule further stated that you had to marry a certain class of relative: either a person from a kinship class of which one member was the mother's brother's daughter, or a person from a kinship class of which one member was your elder sister's daughter (depending on the society or village that you came from). The exogamous rule stated that you had to marry outside your own line. Marriage then is constrained by exogamous and endogamous rules, and serves to legitimize the offspring and give them a *pater* and a *mater*, and bring about an alliance between the groups that exchanged spouses. It should not be forgotten that in all societies marriage is an exchange between groups.

SOME REMARKS ABOUT PLURAL MARRIAGE

Since plural marriage ("bigamy") is a rare occurrence in our own society, indeed a crime, we are not accustomed to thinking of its advantages and disadvantages. Some remarks are in order. First it is never the case that everyone in a polygynous society has more than one wife: were that the case, then the birthrate would have to favor females over males in great disproportion, and in fact, in most societies, more boys than girls are born. Polygyny is achieved either by delaying the age at marriage for males, so that there is a relatively larger number of (younger) females available for marriage, or by permitting sexual access to the wives of older men on a formal or informal basis. There is no society in the world where sexual access is regularly denied to any large class of people.

On a more mundane level, we might assume that since marriage and sex are so closely linked in our society (thus divorce, until very recently, was only possible on the grounds of "adultery") there would be raging, hair-pulling battles among the women over the man. Mostly this is not the case, and there are a number of ways of handling the stresses involved. Firstly, there may be a senior wife who is the executive officer of the domestic group. She indicates with whom the male will have sex (not excluding herself) and at what time, but also ensuring that each wife shares sufficiently that there is a degree of harmony and peace in the household. Or, there may be a rule that states that the man will visit each wife in turn ("whether he likes it or not") so that none is cheated. Thirdly, there may be some form of institutionalized adultery.

There are societies in which there is cowife hostility, however: we should not get the misleading impression that our intuitions are totally in error.

One good example is the East African tribal group, the Gusii, which has been described by Robert LeVine. The Gusii are patrilineal, and practice polygyny. In Nyasongo, the community where LeVine did an important part of his work, fifteen men are monogamists, eleven men have two wives, and one has three wives. None of the precautionary rules that were suggested in the preceding discussion are followed. The husband sleeps with whomever he pleases: usually the younger or youngest of his wives. Wives are not permitted to have extramarital relations, though husbands are. The wives fear the rejection of the husband, for the only way that they can achieve status in the society is by producing children. Husbands are not punished for refusing to sleep with their wives, and first wives are opposed to their husband's taking a second wife. LeVine reports:

Dissensions among co-wives is one of the most common themes in Gusii folklore. One proverb is: "Another child-bearer is like an ancestor spirit at the outside wall."This is interpreted as meaning that secondary wives bring hatred which can result in murder and invoke the wrath of the spirits. There is a special word, *engareka*, which means "hatred between co-wives."[7]

Dissension is particularly prevalent when the cowives are close in age, for when there is a great disparity in age the younger accepts being ordered about by the older, and in turn expects more "motherly" treatment.

Generally, however, cowives work together, and although they may be subordinate to the husband in "male-dominated" societies, often they form coalitions against the husband to get what they want. In parts of West Africa, women do a lot of trading, and polygyny is positively advantageous, since the husband can be kept content, the children can be looked after, and one of the wives can be freed for trading trips and commercial activity.

I dwell on polygyny, not just because it is so common, but also because Americans and Westerners regard it as some kind of "peculiar" institution. But polygynists, and particularly those who live in extended families, would regard our way as being equally peculiar, and if they learned anthropological jargon might call our society one characterized by serial monogamy and matrifocality, since children stay with the mother (usually) after a divorce, and she takes on a number of husbands, one at a time. They might well comment on the family rows that occur over extramarital affairs, and wonder why we do not adopt polygyny, since that way the hostility is kept within the family, and "the other woman," who pops up so regularly in Ann Landers' advice column, is at least married to the husband.

POLYANDRY

There are a few cases of polyandry in the world: i.e., societies where one woman has a number of husbands. It practially never occurs (there are five recorded cases in Murdock's *Ethnographic Survey*, which is a sample of 862 of the world's cultures).[8]

Sometimes it is almost a casual arrangement, as among the Kadar of South India. Here there were two cases of a woman being shared by two men, but within the same society more men had plural wives, and besides, divorce rates were high, as were remarriages to previous spouses. Although we cannot judge directly, and the ethnographic data is bad, it does not seem too farfetched to suggest that the Kadar were rather casual about household, procreative, and sexual arrangements. Their society was small, they lived in an abundant environment that did not require a tightly organized productive group.

7. Robert LeVine, "Gusii Child Rearing," in *Six Cultures: Studies in Child Rearing*, ed. B. B. Whiting (New York: John C. Wiley & Sons, 1963), p. 41.

8. G. P. Murdock, *World Ethnographic Atlas* (Pittsburgh, Penn.: University of Pittsburgh Press, 1967).

The Toda, on the other hand, are proably the best known and best documented case of polyandry—but it was a special case of polyandry, since the wife was shared between a group of brothers. Thus the term *fraternal polyandry* among the Toda, versus *nonfraternal polyandry* among the Kadar. When the wife was married, she automatically became the wife of the group of brothers, born and unborn, to which her husband belonged. Jealousy seems not to have occurred, although one must always be suspicious of comments such as this, since ethnography tends to be male-biased. Sleeping arrangements were facilitated by having the brother who was engaged in sexual activity leave his cloak outside the door of the bamboo hut which served as dormitory, dairy, and workplace during the day.

I have not discussed every family form and type of marriage in the world because, to be frank, the number and variety of forms that the anthropologist can define is very large. If the social scientist wants to include every different wrinkle, then he or she is going to land up with an enormous number of types. Just to give one example: if you want to distinguish between patrilineal extended households where inheritance passes down the male line to all the children, and patrilineal families where it passes only to one son, then you can use the term "famille souche" for the second case. This is a definitional prob-

lem, and, as a rule, I try to stay out of arguments over definitions because I feel that if it is important for your understanding and research to make fine distinctions and create a number of types, then you should go ahead and do it. If not, then do not. Sometimes we forget, when we get into arguments over whether the X people have extended families or not, that it is we, the anthropologists, who are making up these types, and we should only use them to communicate our data accurately, and as a general rule, use as few definitions as we can get away with.

For Further Reading

Fox, Robin (1967) *Kinship and Marriage*. New York. Penguin Books. This is one of the best and simplest introductions to the study of a central topic in social anthropology, written in a delightful style, clear as a bell.

Bibliography

Buchler, I. R. and Selby, H. A. 1968. *Kinship and Social Organization*. New York: Macmillan.

Gough, Kathleen 1959. "The Nayars and the Definition of Marriage." *Journal of the Royal Anthropological Society* 89.

Murdock, G. P. 1949. *Social Structure*. New York: Macmillan.

5 | Keeping Things Straight in Symbols and Groups

INTRODUCTION

The anthropologist generally takes a much broader view of the structure and workings of human groups than his sociological or psychological colleagues. Sometimes we call our approach the "Man from Mars approach," emphasizing two aspects of our vocation: first, being Martians we bring none of those "taken-for-granted" assumptions about how human beings act together that were mentioned at the end of chapter 2. And second, although we observe the minutiae of everyday behavior when we live in our communities, or with our tribes, we try to draw the broad outlines of the whole society, reconstructing the total organization of people and symbols from our informants' statements, census materials, even questionnaires. In the language of public relations, we tend to go for the "big picture" rather than understand the intricacies of everyday life. The reasons are simple: it is difficult enough in an alien culture, where one usually has less than perfect control of the language and commonsense understandings of the local people to carry out detailed psychological or social psychological research which requires laboratory conditions. We work in natural laboratories, and often these natural laboratories seem to have been constructed by a mad genius to deflect our purposes and distort our results. I ran a psychological scaling task with my Zapotec Indian informants one time, and thought I would go insane as I repeated over and over again the items to be scaled (which they had to memorize, since they were illiterate in the main), with my white file cards with their careful arrangements being blown about the drafty room, pecked at by chickens and turkeys, and turned over by curious children who had never seen their own language written down. Every one of us has a multitude of stories like this. We are generally fairly happy if we can get the broad outlines of the society we are studying, and this is, in the main, what we report.

WHAT IS SOCIAL ORGANIZATION?

Human beings organize themselves (in the sense of the "big picture") in a surprisingly limited number of ways. Every individual everywhere is concerned with getting himself a decent life and livelihood, but everywhere, even among the Ik, there are rules about how to do things properly. Some anthropologists deal specifically with the strugglings and strivings of individuals within the framework of their cultural rules, and they are usually called "decision theorists," or students of "natural decision making." My most recent work has been in this area, but I will postpone its discussion until chapter 7 in favor of the broader approach that examines the rules that structure or define the game that these individuals are playing, and the meanings that the rules embody, or *encode*.

But to answer the question posed by the heading: what is social organization? As I suggested in the first part, it is the shape, form, or configuration that warm bodies take in space and time, like the arrangement of chess pieces on a chessboard. But more importantly for anthropologists, social organization refers to the organization of *symbols* and *ideas*, and how they fit together, or conflict with each other. And finally, the most important thing about symbols is that they are *exchanged*, and they have *value*. The study of social organization can be called the study of the exchange of social symbols, these last being symbols that refer to people.

We often forget that we are engaged in the exchange of symbols because we take it so easily for granted that we can afford to ignore it. A person only thinks about his ability to walk when he stumbles, or breathe when he is choking: those activities are so common as to be largely unnoticed. Similarly, when we think of the idea of "mother," we often forget that it isn't our flesh-and-blood mother that we are talking about who loved us, and who looked after us, and who was unlike any other person in the world; we are speaking of a *class* of women, that is, an idea which has symbolic value. Or consider a wedding, which is a ritual in our own society that is replete with symbolism. It is certainly true that our good friend George, who was our classmate at high school, is marrying Alice, the sock hop queen, and they are warm bodies in space, all right. But more important to the anthropologist is the fact that a wedding is taking place, and, instead of seeing George and Alice (remember, the anthropologist just stepped in off the flight from Mars), he sees two people kneeling together, and is told that

they are "bride" and "groom," and furthermore he is immediately questioned as to whether he is "bride's side" or "groom's side," because they sit on different sides of a place called a church where this thing called a wedding is taking place. Afterwards the "bride" gives the "groom" a ring, and he reciprocates. His informants tell him that the ring symbolizes the perfect symmetric union of the pair, as symbolized by the circular form of the bauble. Then, as the liturgy goes forward, his informant tells him that another exchange is taking place: this time he cannot even see it; it is the exchange of vows. He tape-records it and later, with the help of a trained informant, transcribes and translates it and finds out that the bride is giving sexual and domestic services in return for sustenance and maintenance. He hasn't even seen those functionless silver things that are displayed and represent the repayment of a previous exchange from the newly married couple's parents to some other "relative" or "friend" or a "social debt" which will be repaid at some unspecified later date. These are the wedding gifts, and their symbolic value is emphasized by the fact that they are rarely used, and then only upon ritual occasions. Later he will see the sharing and exchanging of food at the "wedding breakfast," and will be told that people in this culture don't all drink from the same glass, as in many others, but give a token of the same act by clinking their glasses together.

These events, acts, and entities are symbols: food and sex being the most powerful symbols in most cultures, which is not too surprising, since they are the most basic prerequisites for the maintenance of the society and the continuance of the culture.

One of the ways that the anthropologist would characterize American marriages is to use the word *homogamous*, by which he would mean that "like marries like." The reason we can intuit that *homogamy* is a rule in American culture is that *nonhomogamous* marriages make the newspapers, whether they be January-September marriages of an older man with a younger woman, or more rarely vice versa, or whether they be marriages across caste or religious lines—"mixed marriages"—which, as Archie Bunker and clucking dowagers know, "do not work out." One of the *negotiations* that take place before, during, and after marriages concerns the intricacies of the "homogamy game," which is played by all parties to the marriage: husband-wife, the two immediate families of both, and the kindreds on either side. Of course one marries for love, but it's easier to love people like· yourself than people who are very different.[1] The "homogamy rule" is another way of stating the rule of endogamy, and is never explicitly stated in American culture: there is no law requiring it, and such laws (such as the infamous miscegenation statutes) as this have been declared unconstitutional. But it's a rule, nevertheless, implicit in the way that Americans, English, and western Europeans think, talk, and act when it comes to marriage.

The other thing that the anthropologist would inquire about was the relationship between that husband and wife before marriage, and he would discover that they weren't relatives. Most Westerners believe that close relatives should not marry, even though they don't talk about the rules of *exogamy*, the way the anthropologist does. The rule is so taken-for-granted that we practically never talk about it, except to counsel our children that they cannot marry their siblings (brothers and sisters), for reasons that are never really explained except sometimes to say that the babies would all be deformed. Exogamous prescriptions vary from state to state in the United States, and in my local (Canadian) culture they extended to first cousins, who

were defined as the children of the full brothers or sisters of one's parents.

Another rule in American culture for spouse choice is that there aren't any rules (supposedly). One marries for "love," and "love" is a powerful symbol in American culture, since it is the binding force that keeps families and marriages together and creates social stability at the domestic level. Spouses are free to decide to marry, and (again supposedly) the only people who are immediately concerned are the families of the marrying pair. And American culture is unusual in the sense that the exchange that takes place in marriage is sharply limited. For example, no explicit named kinship relationship is set up between the parents of the marrying pair: they refer to each other *teknonymously,* that is, by tracing the relationship to each other through their children: Alice's folks talk about their affines as "George's family."

ANOTHER HOMOGAMOUS CASE: BINT 'AMM MARRIAGE

A very nice contrast with homogamous marriage in Western European countries is the marriage customs of people of the Middle East, where homogamy is also practiced. Here the exogamous rule states that you cannot marry your full brother or sister (unless you are an ancient Pharoah), but that you should marry and are encouraged, induced, and pressured into marrying a very close "brother" or "sister" who is a member of your own group and is drawn from a pool of spouses one member of whom is one's father's brother's child. This is called *patrilateral parallel cousin*

1. There is a good deal of sociological and psychological work on the subject of homogamy, which seems silly to the anthropologists, because their colleagues in other disciplines seem to think that they are discovering some eternal verity, whereas the anthropologists "know" that they are just studying the impact of a cultural rule of people's exchange system.

marriage because the marrying pair are patrilateral parallel cousins. Patrilateral, because they trace their relationship through their respective fathers. Think for a moment: if I marry my father's brother's daughter, then she is marrying her father's brother's son. Parallel, because the person I marry is a child of a sibling of the same sex as my linking parent (i.e., my mother's sister's child and my father's brother's child are both *parallel cousins*). If the person I married were the child of a sibling of the opposite sex of my linking parent, then I could be marrying my *cross cousin* (i.e. my mother's brother's child and my father's sister's child are my *cross cousins*). It is as close as one can come in human society to marrying a sister. These marriages are often called "endogamous marriages," and the system of group alignment that takes place as a result of such marriages is called endogamous systems. Now this can be confusing because, as I stated earlier, every system of marriage is endogamous, i.e., has boundaries, but the reason the term is applied to the Middle Eastern case is because marriage takes place *within* the group; and the group in this case is the *patrilineage*.

But there seems to be a contradiction here. Recall, if you will, the discussion about incest and the dispute between Freud and Westermarck. Westermarck's hypothesis that we have a "natural" sexual lack of interest in our sisters and all people of opposite sex with whom we were raised seems to be invalidated by the practice of patrilateral parallel cousin marriage. But in fact, a close look seems to support Westermarck's thesis that "distance lends enchantment," because great care is taken in Middle Eastern society to keep the sexes apart. In traditional communities, women are secluded, kept away from the men, and the novelty that was spoken of as being linked to sexual arousal is maintained artificially, by a cultural ruse. Some work that Robert Fernea and I did indicated that

where you found a high degree of seclusion, you would find also that these marriages were durable. If seclusion was not so marked, you either found a reduction in the number of patrilateral parallel cousin marriages or a rise in the frequency of divorce.

A NOTE ON GROUPS

In the American case we used two terms that referred to the groups that were involved in the marriage: the immediate family and the kindred (or better, the "relatives on each side"). In the Middle Eastern case we observe that there is a different way of defining the group—a way that is found in a plurality of societies in the world; that is, the *patrilineage*. This is a group of people who are recruited to a well-defined group at birth by emphasizing the tie between *men*, rather than women, or rather than both. The use of the word "lineage" emphasizes the metaphor of a vertical line of men around whom the group is organized. In traditional genealogical diagrams we represent men as triangles and women as circles, so we can diagram to "core" or the patrilineage as a line of men in the following way:

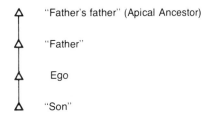

"Father's father" (Apical Ancestor)

"Father"

Ego

"Son"

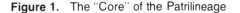

Figure 1. The "Core" of the Patrilineage

Symbolic essences are passed down the line of men: in this case it is that bundle of symbols which we can abbreviate as "membership in the group." This symbolic bundle passes through all men from an ancestor at the top of the line, the *apical* ancestor, and is transmitted *through* all men to their descendants, and to all women, where it stops. In the following lineage, I will mark those members of the group who are in the lineage, by darkening the symbol for male and female, and leaving undarkened those who are not members of the lineage, and you will notice immediately that membership passes through the lineage, like electricity through an open circuit, but only to the women where it is blocked (the circuit is closed).

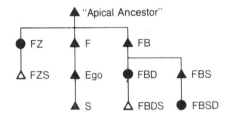

Figure 2. A Patrilineal Group

Now the "depth" of patrilineages varies from society to society, and indeed from community to community. In some Arab societies the depth can reach up to fifteen generations before it fades off into mythical history: people can keep track of all their patrilineal relatives going back fifteen generations. In other societies the patrilineages are only remembered going back four generations. And membership in lineages is sometimes manipulated and *negotiated* in order to accord with the present state of affairs: that is, marriages that were wrong originally become right with the passage of time by conveniently transplanting the genealogical position of some in-marrying member (or whole family) into one's own line by a collusive act of collective amnesia. The logic, which has been studied in the Middle East, Africa, and New Guinea, seems to go as follows: "If so-and-so" married "such-and-so" umpteen generations ago, they must have

been members of the same group, since they were man and wife, and so the genealogies shall be brought into line with the rule. In a word, there is a cover-up: the rule is maintained and the society agrees to the change.

DUALISM

The reason anthropologists became fascinated by endogamous systems was because they seemed anomalous, since they were not found anywhere else in the world. The rest of the world works on a *binary* principle of "in-group" versus "out-group," and the solidarity of the society is based on the exchange of symbols between these groups. In Middle Eastern marriage systems there is most certainly an exchange of symbols: in tangible terms, ."bride wealth" in the form of cattle, sheep, or goats is paid by the father of the groom to the bride's family, and they in turn furnish a trousseau for the bride in the form of rugs, blankets, and a few other household items. Dualism, or binarism—the widespread practice of defining symbols, and in particular social symbols, by contrasting or "opposing" them—is found throughout the system of symbolic meanings linked with the distinction between men and women. Take the symbolic layout of the Berber house, which Bordieu has described.[2]

The Berber house is the world of women, at the same time as it (with the garden) is the world of all that is sacred and licit. The world outside of the house is the man's world: men who stay in the house are regarded as nonmen: they are like brood hens, staying at home during the day when they should be outside in the fields, or at the assembly house. When boys mature they

2. P. Bordieu, "The Berber House or the World Reversed," in *Mélanges Offerts à Claude Lévi-Strauss*, ed. J. Pouillon and P. Maranda (Paris: Mouton, 1971).

must leave the world of women, and leave the house with the father.

The interior of the house is saturated in symbols which relate to men and women. It is divided in two: the upper part (facing north) is the domain of light, the fireplace, the loom, the place of women's activity, and the lower, dark part of the house, the place of death, sexual activity, germination of the seed, birth, and rebirth. The weaving loom alone summarizes the way stations of a woman's life, her umbilical cord is buried beneath it, she is made to pass through the warp of the loom magically to protect her virginity. At marriage she moves from behind (the protection of) the loom to be in front of it, symbolizing the passage of her honor from her father's and brothers' keeping to that of her husband. In the fire burn the embers, which symbolize in their turn the womb of the mother with its secret hidden fire.

At the center of the dividing wall, male and female meet. The beam across the top of the main pillar is male, and it rests on the trunk, which is female. Around the beam is coiled the snake, the symbol of male fertility, but the pillar supports the beam, and "stands, but has no feet."

The house is the place of women: "Woman has only two dwellings," says the proverb, "the house and the tomb." But although the house is "hers," it symbolizes the opposition between male and female, and their conjunction. The oppositions come in a series:

fire	water
cooked	raw
high	low
light	shadow
day	night
male	female
fertilizing	able to be fertilized
culture	nature

The series, through its logical arrangement "keeps things straight."

So, in endogamous systems we find that however much one may marry a brother or sister, the distinction between "my group" and "other group" which is denied in the system of marriage, is recreated in the world of activities and in the arrangement of the symbols of the house.

VARIATIONS ON THE THEME OF DUALISM:

(1) Unconscious, Egocentric Dualism

Dualism turns up as an organizing principle in human societies all over the world, and in a variety of different forms. Some societies bask in unconscious dualism, like the Zapotec communities I studied for the past nine years. Here the two groups are not named by the villagers, and, like our homogamous marriage "rules," are denied in statements like the following: "Here we are one happy village, peaceful and tranquil, where we all regard ourselves as brothers," which is strictly untrue, and comes out most clearly in the two most important topics in their lives, sex and witchcraft. Any village elder will tell you, for example, that there is a rule that states that sexual intercourse ought to take place exclusively between husband and wife in a monogamous union. But adultery goes on continually. Confronted by the facts, the village elder will proceed: "Ah, but there are heavy punishments for adultery; the adulterous wife should be beaten by her husband." (Wife beating is a semiritualistic form of assault, where the man grabs the woman by her hair and swings her around, landing a few glancing blows on her face and body, all the while setting up a caterwauling wail that attests to his moral probity, while the woman quietly keens away.) "And," the village elder continues, "a man who is adulterous will be reprimanded by his godfather, jailed, and fined." And these statements are true, all right, and they operate some of the time. And the time when they apply is when a woman (or man) has an affair with an "outsider," or, in the local terminology, a "person who lives far away from you," which translates as "a person who is neither kin, fictive kin (godparent/godchild), or neighbor."

This is a nice case, and unusual, because we can see the operation of rules that contradict each other. The exogamous rule states that one must marry an outsider, and the incest rule prohibits sexual relations with kin as close as first cousin; whereas the extramarital sex rule (unconscious, unlike the incest rule) states that you cannot have affairs with those whom you could marry. The reasoning seems to be philosophical. Central to the Zapotec villagers' world is the division of the community into insiders and outsiders. Sexual intercourse is a symbol of the inside par excellence, and so if you have an incestuous relationship with an insider that is all right, in the sense that you do not attack the fundamental unconscious ordering of the social categories, but if you openly, publicly have an affair with an outsider, you are taking an inside symbol and applying it to the outside. You are turning the organization of the unconscious world upside down.

The same logic applies to witch-finding procedures. When I was first in the community where I did most of my work, I wanted to interview the witches because I was interested in deviance. So I went looking for them. The family I was living with trusted me enough to tell me that there were witches in the community, but that practically all of them lived on the other side of the village. Luckily, I had a good friend who lived right in the middle of this coven, and I asked him discreetly about the witches, and to my chagrin he pointed out that practically all of them lived up where I was living. No one was lying: witches are drawn from those people who (in the local terms) "live far away from one."

Now, in the case of the village Zapotec,

dualism is fundamental to their way of thinking, but it is an *egocentric* dualism in that everyone has their own list of witches and everyone has their own group of outsiders. And they do not appear to be aware of this: they do not compare notes, as it were. And it doesn't turn up in such an explicit form that they can tell you about it; it is unconscious. It is always very important to "keep things straight."

(2) The Akwe-Shavante: Conscious, Society-Wide Dualism

If we travel from the Highlands of Southern Mexico into the scrublands of Central Brazil and look at a remote tribe studied by David Maybury-Lewis called the Akwe-Shavante, we find the same state of affairs, but different.[3]

The Shavante guard the philosophical foundations of their social order, just as the Zapotec do. Their word for incest is the same as the word that is used in their legends to refer to the change of people into animals, and vice versa. In both the Zapotec and the Shavante case, there is a strong emphasis on *maintaining* the distinctions between things, or keeping their categories straight, and since incest would foul up the distinction between in-group and out-group, they label it for what it is: a dehumanizing, or "de-Shavante-izing" process, just like the change from a human being to an animal, or from nature to culture.[4]

3. For the best and most candid account of what it is like to do field work, and what relations are like between informants and the anthropologist, read *The Savage and The Innocent* by David Maybury-Lewis. And if you want to contrast the Akwe-Shavante with a people not too dissimilar to the Zapotec, read *Crazy February*, a novel by Carter Wilson. Both are available in paperback.

4. In explaining the importance of "keeping things straight" in society, I have often used the *analogy* of the individual's experiences with psychedelic drugs as an illustration to my students.

Maybury-Lewis's analysis of Shavante led him to postulate that there were bundles of "analogical antitheses" that ran throughout Shavante thinking about Shavante sociology, to keep things straight. He lists them:

HOUSEHOLD

Those Married In	Dominant Lineage
Outsiders	Insiders
Subordinate	Superordinate

COMMUNITY

They	We
Opposite Faction	My Faction

RELATIONSHIP

They	We

TERMINOLOGY

Marriageable	Nonmarriageable

COSMOLOGY

Wazepari'wa	Spirits of the Dead
Affines	Kin
Wasi're'wa	Waniwihā[5]

I can better explain what is meant by these dualistic antitheses if we look at them in order.

1. *Household*

Boys marry into their wives' households. Because of polygyny, there is a wide disparity in the ages of the husband and wife—the boy marries a girl who may be a babe-in-arms as soon as he enters the age-grade that leaves the bachelor's hut. He is embarrassed by any suggestion that he might be having sexual intercourse with his wife, not because she is so young, for defloration can take place as early as when the girl has reached the age of eight. He is embarrassed because it would be an admission that he was committing himself to residence with his in-laws, in a house where he is a stranger and a member of the (patrilineal) out-group. The more he is "married," the more he has to come under the authority of his father-in-law, and work for him. In his father's house he is a

member of the in-group. Maybury-Lewis describes the time when the chief was building a house and the whole family moved in with the anthropologist. Two things struck him: first, how fast the young married couple moved out, to get away from the in-laws and establish a proper distance between them (normally they are separated by a screen in the girl's father's house); and second, how the patrilineal kinsmen of the bride lounged about helping little, if at all, since they would have to go to work in their wives' fathers' houses, and they were very much "at home" here, in their own house. These are some of the symbols that Maybury-Lewis sums up by contrasting "those married in" versus "dominant lineage," "outsiders" versus "insiders," "subordinate" versus "superordinate."[6]

2. *Community*

The community is divided into two sides, called *waniwihā* and *wasi're'wa*, respectively. These two words are hard to translate: some would render them "kin" vs. "affine," but they seem to come closer

---

In the early sixties drugs like LSD were called "psychotomimetic" drugs because they were thought to mimic psychotic states of mind. Ingesting these drugs caused subjects to confound the basic categorical distinctions between objects. The world was seen as continuous (which, of course, it is) rather than chopped up into categories. The flower would melt into the table, one sense would be interpreted by another (you could "hear" the flower). From my reading on psychosis, in particular accounts of the onset of psychosis, it seems clear that the human mind tries desperately to hold on to the categorical distinctions of everyday life, whether they are conscious or unconscious. When subjects can no longer do this, they experience tremendous anxiety. Remember, this is an analogy, because we are now talking about groups of people and their negotiated realities, both conscious and unconscious, which are expressed in symbols and the organization of symbols.

5. David Maybury-Lewis, *Akwe-Shavante Society* (London: Oxford University Press, 1974), p. 299.

6. Ibid.

to being what the Zapotec call "people who live close to me," or more in Shavante, "my people" versus "others." Unlike the Zapotec there are social devices (patrilineages) which help the Shavante divide up their community. The lineages are well-defined (unlike our kindred and the Zapotec "people who live close to me") and are named. Lineages are formed into factions, and thus create the distinction between "my faction" and "opposite faction." People of the speaker's faction are called *wasiwadi*, to distinguish them from people of his own lineage, who are addressed by appropriate kinship terms. Witchcraft (as in Zapotec) is a political act directed against "others," but contrary to Zapotec, the whole process is out in the open and consciously developed.

3. Kin Terminology

The kinship terminology reflects the underlying binary division of the world into two: reflecting the distinction between *waniwihã* and *wasi're'wa*. Once again, in contrast to Zapotec, who have no kin terms for "people who live far away" except to say "they are nothing to me," the terminological system of the Shavante consciously includes the separation of kinsmen into "them" and "us." "We" marry "them." Unlike Zapotec, adultery seems unimportant to Shavante, but when it occurs the relationship must be with either an outsider or a member of one's *wasi're'wa*. Brother's wife in Zapotec is felt to be a particularly desirable sex partner, perhaps because it is so incestuous. Somewhat the same occurs in Shavante; but then the brother's wife is an outsider, a member of another lineage and a *wasi're'wa*, whereas in Zapotec she is an insider and sexual relations are incestuous.

4. Cosmology

Dyadic relationships turn up "on the ground" but they also turn up "in heaven" as well. The system of meanings that is found in the categories of social organization (organization of social symbols) extends quite readily into other symbolic arenas, just as it did in Berber houses. In the cosmological system, the major distinction is between the *wazepari'wa*, who are dangerous spirits associated with one's affines, and the *da hiebá*, who are the benevolent spirits of the dead.[7] And Maybury-Lewis summarizes the opposed characteristics in the cosmological system briefly:

wazepari'wa	da hiebá
malevolence	benevolence
taking	giving
terrifying	consoling
ending	beginning
(death?)	(life?)
west	east
affinal place	kin place
affines	kin
wasi're'wa	waniwihã[8]

Each symbol is defined by the other and opposed to it, just as black is defined by white and opposed to it in the Western scheme of color categories. Symbols cannot stand alone: they are arranged in orders and structures, the simplest one being binary opposition. Binary opposition is found worldwide and serves to "keep things straight." I have described two societies where it prevails in the ordering of social symbols. They are the same, but different. The Zapotec are largely unaware and have practically no words for the binary oppositions they live by, whereas the Shavante do have words for them and are more conscious of their existence. In Shavante the two opposed groups are fixed

7. The opposition between kin and affines, which is expressed in aggression and hostility in political life, is "exorcised in heaven" (in Maybury-Lewis's words) where the rather nasty features of one's affines are overborne by their status as dead people. The only good affine is a dead affine.

8. Maybury-Lewis, *Akwe-Shavante Society*, p. 292.

in membership by recruitment to a patrilineage at birth, and by membership in a faction. It is out in the open and stable. But each Zapotec family has its own set of outsiders and witches. Membership is unfixed and constantly changing. Yesterday you might have been one of my witch candidates, but today, out of the blue, you asked me to be your godparent. People who are godparents are *never* outsiders so your status as a witch candidate vanished, overnight. We can therefore distinguish between the Zapotec's egocentric dualism and the Shavante's society-wide dualism.

RECIPROCAL DUALISM: THE KARIERA SYSTEM

The epitome of systems of dualistic reciprocity is to be found in Australia, and we can briefly describe one simple case—the Kariera.

There are three ways that one can describe the Kariera system depending on what one wants to emphasize. One can call it a system of restricted *exchange*, emphasizing that there are only two sides that make up the whole society, "our side," or "our skin," and "other skin." Or one can call them systems of symmetric alliance, emphasizing that the symbols of the same value are exchanged back and forth between the two sides. Or one can emphasize the terminological code (i.e., the names for important social categories) and the system of marriage, and call it a system of *bilateral cross-cousin marriage*. *Bilateral* in that there is a category of people who are cousins on both my father's and my mother's side simultaneously and *cross cousin* because this bilateral cousin is simultaneously my father's sister's child *and* my mother's brother's child.

Try to draw a diagram of the relationships that would have to obtain between people who were arranged in two sides. Do it in patrilineages both for the sake of simplicity and ethnographic accuracy. Re-

member this when a man marries someone who is simultaneously his mother's brother's child and father's sister's child. To save you hours, here is how it all falls out:

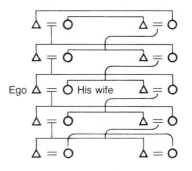

Figure 3. Kariera Kinship Diagram

Remember that this is a diagram of *positions*, not people. Students always ask, "What happens if Ego doesn't have a person who is simultaneously his FZD/MBD who can become his W?" He'll get married; the system is much more flexible than it looks, because what that diagram displays are the *rules* of the system, the "skins" or sides, the relationships of sister-exchange (my group gives your group a woman (or a man, it doesn't matter), and your group gives one to my group), and the kinship terminology reflects this fact. Since a lot of these systems were polygynous, a usual ruse was utilized to guarantee that every man got a wife—just as in Shavante, the man married a woman who was much younger than he was. But even this was flexible; except under extreme circumstances, young men are not going to wait around for an extended period after puberty until they can have legitimate sexual relations with a woman. An Australian, Waipuldanya by name, who lived in a more complex system than the Kariera, but one which embodied the precise same principles, explained it:

37

Soon after she [i.e., his future wife] was born, her maternal uncle, Gurukul, said to Jupiter: "Here is the wife of Waipuldanya."

But aboriginal law, inflexible as it is in many respects, is tolerant in others.

When I was twenty years old Nora was still a child, unready for marriage. I would have to wait five years for her, and the tribe, meanwhile, would be wasting the procreative power of one of its young men, thus impairing its own chance of survival. In such a situation the Elders were alert for a compromise—and they soon found one.

Her name was Hannah Dulban, of the Ngamayang skin and the Wandarang tribe.

It wasn't easy.

When an aboriginal uncle searches for a wife for his Nibarli ["son"] he is not concerned with such trivia as her appearance, her disposition or her accomplishments. Beauty, fripperies, temper, and culinary art are subordinate to the primary question: Is she Right-Side?

In most tribes there is an arbitrary division of men and women into groups known as "skins" which indicate tribal and inter-tribal relationships. I am of the Bungadi skin, although my father is a Burlangban. My six daughters are also Burlangban . . . .

It is a grave offense, subject to severe punishment, to marry into any skin-group which is Wrong-Side . . . .

The aborigines believe that the marriage of incompatible skins may lead to imbecility, paralysis, and other physical and mental deficiencies . . . .The skin-group system automatically precludes me from marrying any closer relative than my cousin's daughter's daughter.[9]

CONCLUSION

Dualistic, or dyadic systems, are found all over the world, although Australia and North and South America furnish particularly good examples of them. They are generally found in small populations: either small endogamous communities or small tribal units of up to about 2,000 people. Everywhere that Waipuldanya went in his treks as a medical aide, he found brothers-in-law, fathers, mothers, grandfathers, nephews, nieces, and so on.

Because kinship presupposes reciprocity and balanced exchanges, and because people all over the world use kinship to theorize about their social worlds, anthropologists have emphasized the balance and symmetry of these systems, but we should not be fooled by them. In Shavante the symmetric system was overturned by a system of factionalism, which included murder and sorcery as part of the political process. In Australia, where the balance is supposedly perfect, the politics of polygyny were practiced to the point of older men trying to gain wives and prestige at the expense of the younger men. Among the Sharanahua, a group of Peruvian Indians who live in a remote region by the Brazilian border, Janet Siskind found that the politics of hunting and sex were markedly asymmetrical and unbalanced, even though we can characterize the people as "dualistic." The Sharanahua are opposite from the Berber in that sexual antagonism is open, despite complementarity of roles, and sex is the engine that "drives" the hunting economy. Successful hunters have more wives, more mistresses, and more prestige than unsuccessful hunters. And, as Siskind points out, all of this is culturally induced: there is neither a shortage of game, or fish, or roots, or women, except that they make it so. The lineage is supposed to be solidary but, since brothers share the same incest taboo,

9. Because I dislike writers (and talkers) who do not finish their stories, I can disclose that it all turned out right in the end. A woman was found, and although no right-thinking aboriginal would care about fripperies, . . ."Hannah was attractive by all aboriginal standards: maiden's firm breasts, rounded abdomen, strong thighs, large eyes with long lashes, broad lashes, full lips, and flashing teeth revealed by a spontaneous smile which broke without cause into melting feminine laughter." Waipuldanya, *I, the Aboriginal* (New York: World, 1970), p. 108.

they chase the same women, and competition over women is intense. Siskind indicates that despite their protestations, the Sharanahua have a myth (shared with many South American hunting tribes):

The central theme describes a love affair between a tapir and a woman. The husband eventually discovers his wife and her tapir lover, kills the tapir and, in many versions, forces his wife to eat or copulate with the tapir's penis, after which she dies. This theme appears in two Sharanahua myths ...with additional complications. In this myth the tapir, the largest game animal in the forest, is literally connected with women. Man in the role of hunter kills his rival, who becomes meat, eliminates freely given sex from the universe, and sets up an antagonistic relationship to women, in which the hunter must win women by killing game.[10]

Thus within systems of balance and reciprocity we find systems of competition, rivalry, and struggle for power and prestige. The harmonious balance that is suggested by the word reciprocity is belied in most dualistic societies by politics and ambition, envy and aggression. The problem of keeping the society together is established in the rules of descent and marriage. The problems of keeping the society going, of leaving room within the society for the person to express himself, of leaving options for different kinds of people who want to make a better life for themselves are solved in the symbolic asymmetries that all dualistic societies exhibit.

SUMMARY

We have been concerned in this chapter with binarism in its social guise: dualistic, or dyadic societies. I presented four examples which exhibited four ways in which dyadic principles are worked out in ethnographic cases: (1) the Middle Eastern ("endogamous") case, where the dualisms

were of a symbolic nature, concerned the place of men and women, as in the example of the Berber house; (2) the case of "unconscious dualism," where the Zapotec carefully chose his witch candidates, and his illicit sex partners on dualistic principles that he or she was unaware of; (3) the Shavante case, where the dualisms were explicit, conscious, and pervaded the organization of social symbols; and (4) the Kariera case, where kinship terms, marriage, group formation and exchange fitted together in a neat compact package. Another theme ran throughout the chapter was that reciprocity and symmetry are represented in the system of rules, but that competition, rivalry, and antagonism appeared in other parts of the social and symbolic system.

For Further Reading

Bates, Daisy (1973) *The Passing of the Aborigines*. Pocket Books, New York. Ms. Bates was an extraordinary, Edwardian woman who spent a lifetime among the Australian aborigines, and probably understood them better than any other European. A marvellous ethnography, by a wonderful woman who helped most of the best anthropologists who worked in Australia, but whose story is more accurate than theirs.

Maybury-Lewis, David (1968) *The Savage and the Innocent*. Boston. Beacon Books. One of the most candid and realistic accounts of what it is like to do field work among a difficult, inaccessible tribe. If you have ever wondered where that data comes from, you will have a much better idea from reading this delightful honest book.

Siskind, Janet (1973) *To Hunt in the Morning*. New York. Oxford Press. An ecological study of a dualistic society, beautifully written, intelligent reading.

10. Janet Siskind, *To Hunt in the Morning* (New York: Oxford Press, 1973), p. 104.

SOCIAL ORGANIZATION: SYMBOL, STRUCTURE, AND SETTING
Keeping Things Straight in Symbols and Groups

Bibliography

Douglas, Mary 1966. *Purity and Danger.* London: Routledge and Kegan Paul.

Radcliffe-Brown, A. R. and Forde, D. eds. *African Systems of Kinship and Marriage.* Oxford: International African Institute.

6 | Asymmetric Systems

Human beings expend a lot of time "keeping things straight." One method that I discussed is to set up a system of related oppositions: black-white, holy-unholy, male-female, inside-outside, and so on. This is the kind of binary reckoning that computers do fairly well, but that human beings through their infinite capacity of extension of meaning through metaphor, metonymy, association, and imagination can do much better.

But it is not the only way of keeping things straight: another way to do it is to create a scale, or measuring stick of some kind, and order things with it. The ordinary ruler is the most powerful measuring instrument we have. All other measures are based on it, surprising as that may seem. This is because it has a zero point, regular intervals, and can be related to a special set of numbers called the "reals." So if you want to order some set of elements, the best way to do it is to measure them: you can take an infinitely countable set of lengths and apply them to a corresponding number of long objects, and you have them nicely sorted, and "kept straight."

No human social organization is based on such a powerful measuring principle. But there is a weaker form of measure that is very commonly used, and that is the "preference order," which in mathematical symbols is given by ">," which you will recognize from high school math. The usual notation used for social or economic data is slightly different, "$\succ$," which can mean "is preferred to," "is more powerful than," "is more holy than," or "is of higher status than."

Now every schoolboy knows (as the historian Macaulay used to say just before he developed some particularly difficult point) that if A>B and B>C, then A>C. When this property holds true of three or more elements (social categories, in the upcoming), it is called a *transitive* relationship, or a relationship of *transitivity*. When, on the other hand, the statement $A \succ B$, $B \succ C$, $C \succ A$ is true (and notice we cannot use the mathematical symbol because it would be strictly false), we say that the relationship is *intransitive* or characterized by *intransitivity*. Intransitivity is not rare in human thinking—to the constant irritation of psychologists and microeconomic theorists who would prefer that people could keep things straight in a "proper way." People often cannot remember their preferences, or find that the criteria for judging things are so complex that they cannot be reduced to a simple (unidimensional) ordering. I myself, for example, would prefer a year off to a grant of $10,000.00, and would prefer a grant of ten thousand dollars to membership in a tightly organized research trip to an exotic tribe, and would prefer a tightly organized research trip to an exotic tribe to a year off. The reasons are complicated but the ordering is intransitive. Intransitives certainly occur in our thinking.

INTRANSITIVITY OF PREFERENCE ORDERING IN HUMAN SOCIETY

The beauty of intransitivity in ordering human societies is that there is no bottom, no *pariah group* that is lower than any other group, just as there is no person or group who is top-dog, clearly dominant over all. Americans are very good at preference ordering occupations, for example, and, when regularly asked to do so by sociologists, give very reliable and valid orderings. This means that they give the same answers to the same questions and that there is a high degree of agreement among different people. Imagine then, a system of occupations where people said that a brain surgeon was preferred to a college professor, a college professor to a sanitation worker, and a sanitation worker to a brain surgeon. And the brain surgeons concurred in this judgment, as did the college professors and the sanitation men. Think what it would do to a marriage system if there was a rule of *hypergamy* (that is, a rule that states that a woman should marry into a higher status group). No sanitation man would ever let his daughter marry a brain surgeon, just as no brain surgeon would let his daughter marry a college professor, and so on. Similarly, if there was a rule of *hypogamy* (that is, a rule that states that a woman should marry into a lower status group), the cycle would be reversed. And in neither case would we find a bottom or a top to the system, but rather a set of cycles of exchange which incorporate the very powerful sorting device or preference ordering, and avoid the creation of a hierarchical class or caste structure.

This kind of marriage system is found all over the world, particularly in Asia, and it can get very complicated indeed. Just as with dualistic systems, we can refer to these systems of marriage in three ways: (1) systems of generalized exchange; (2) systems of asymmetric alliance; and (3) systems of matrilateral cross-cousin marriage. If we focus on the fact that more than two groups, in fact any number of groups, can be incorporated into the marriage cycles of symbolic exchange, then we use the term "generalized exchange." If we want to focus on the fact that instead of reciprocity (i.e., A gives a sister or brother to B, who returns in kind), we have A giving a brother or sister to B who gives a brother or sister to C who gives in kind to A (in the simplest formulation), then we use the term asymmetric alliance. If we want to emphasize the kinship category from which the wife (in this case) is drawn, then we use the expression matrilateral cross-cousin marriage, because the engine that keeps this general system of exchange going is a restrained spouse choice drawing from a class, one member of which will be MBD.

The simplest example of such a system would incorporate three lineages (we shall use patrilineages, since they are more commonly found in these systems, but any kind of social category or local group can serve). We get a simplified schematic chart of the various positions as follows:

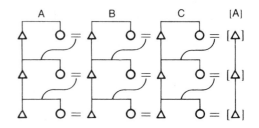

Figure 4. Matrilateral Cross-Cousin Marriage

The "=" means "is married to" and the wavy descending lines are lines from parents to children, and the horizontal lines link brother and sister. Note that every man on the second and third horizontal line is married to his "mother's brother's daughter," and every woman (conversely) to her "father's sister's son."

Notice also that women flow in the same direction, from left to right. A "gives a woman to" B, who "gives a woman to" C, who "gives a woman to" A, and the circle is complete. (For this reason some people call these systems "marriage in a circle," or *circular connubium*.) In the Kariera example, A gave to B, who gave back to A, and there was neither circle nor cycle; just reciprocity.

Systems of this kind, particularly when they utilize preference orderings, can keep a lot of people straight, many more than the 2,000 or so upper limit that is imposed by dualistic systems. I do not know what the upper limit is, but it is certainly above 100,000. And remember, you don't have to marry your mother's brother's daughter, you have to marry a "proper woman," a "potential spouse," and that can mean a lot of different things depending on the differing ethnographic circumstances. It's a fact that if everyone *had* to marry their mother's brother's daughter, then there would be a lot of unmarried people, since it is very hard on biological principles to guarantee that each mother's brother's daughter will be available for every father's sister's son. Differential fertility, child mortality, and the laws of probability will take care of that. So any tribe that might have insisted on strict adherence to the rule of marrying your true mother's brother's daughter would lose out in the evolutionary scramble for reproductive success.

In the large scale, the system works out well because it keeps groups ordered (related and in place) and creates stable alliances together with constant cycles of symbolic exchange.[1] These cycles of symbolic exchange link intermarrying groups as "wife-givers" and "wife-takers," thus generalizing the distinction between "kin" and "affine" that we noted in Shavante and Sharanahua. Instead of a man choosing a spouse from "other side," he chooses a spouse from a group where his own group chose one in the past, or from some other group, provided that his own group has not given a spouse to them in the past. Sometimes the logic is carried further, as in South India, where there are special relationships with the wife-givers of my wife-givers, and those groups are proscribed as well. If you combine this generalized form of exchange with polygynous marriage practice, widow inheritance by the son, then the complexity increases, but in theory and in the local practice all the categories of kinfolk and groups is kept straight. Faron studied a number of reservations of the Araucanian-

1. The exchange of human beings is probably the most powerful form that exchange can take, which is why anthropologists have concentrated on them. But we should remember that the spouse *is* a symbol, and by no means the only symbol that is exchanged. Lévi-Strauss (1969) instances W. R. Head's (1917) description of the gifts that are given by the groom's family to the bride's family when Haka Chin marries within their own village, that is, in the simplest case. There are five major gifts. One small part of one of them is as follows, in Lévi-Strauss's words: "It [the *mante*, or little payment, which is one of the three parts of the *ni man*, or aunt's payment] is as follows: (1) the aunt escorts her niece to the husband's house and demands a knife, because it is thought that she must have used her own to cut her way through the forest; (2) the aunt asks for a bead for going inside the enclosure of the bridegroom's house; (3) she receives a gift for climbing the outside ladder; (4) she receives some iron for 'licking the iron,' a ritual of friendship; (5) she is given a mat for sitting down in the house and (6) a cup, for offering drink to those who have discussed the price with her; (7) she must now be presented with other propitiatory gifts to dissuade her from returning home with her niece, and be given in addition: (8) coral beads; (9) a copper belt; (10) a rug to replace the one she wore out in carrying her niece when she was a baby; (11) a pig; (12) a special payment for having drunk outside the village with the husband and his family."

speaking Mapuche Indians who apparently have created a generalized system in the recent past (there is some evidence that in the early colonial period they practiced bilateral cross-cousin marriage, or reciprocal exchange), and he models the system in a simple map to show the direction of the flow of women, and it looks like this:

arguments took place over the organization of one such group of about 200 Purum, members of an Old Kuki tribe of Manipur, and the matrilateral system does work with one qualification—everyone must be married.

We can simplify the Purum data so that it reflects three intermarrying groups: with women "flowing" from *A* to *B*, to *C*, and

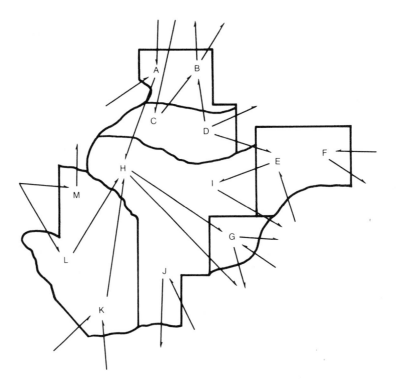

Figure 5. Flow of Women on Six Mapuche Reservations[2]

The wife-giving and receiving groups are patrilineages here, as is commonly found.

But what about small communities? Does matrilateral exchange work there as well? In small communities one would expect the problems posed by demography and the unequal size of sibling sets, as well as the unequal size of groups. Raging

back to *A* again. If there were 141 couples, then the table that represented the matrilateral exchange system would look like the following:

2. Louis Faron, "Mapuche Social Structure," *Illinois Studies in Anthropology* (Urbana, Ill.: University of Illinois Press, 1961).

TABLE ONE

IDEAL REPRESENTATION OF MATRILATERAL EXCHANGE

		Women of	
	A	B	C
Men of A	0	47	0
Men of B	0	0	47
Men of C	47	0	0

Put zeros on the diagonal of the matrix to ensure that no one marries into their own group, and then allocate the marriages in the way described.

Now look at the way the marriages actually distribute:

TABLE TWO

DISTRIBUTION OF MARRIAGES IN PURUM

		Women of	
	A	B	C
Men of A	0	1	26
Men of B	23	16	21
Men of C	0	52	2

It certainly looks as though people are regularly breaking the rule sufficiently often to make us doubt that there is a rule at all. It looks like men of A are taking women from C and giving women to B, which is as it should be. Men of C are taking women from B, but are giving them to both A and B (as well as a couple to C), which is not proper at all. Men of B are taking women from everyone, and giving them back to C and to a lesser extent to B. So how can we possibly say that there is a matrilateral system operating? Quite simply by requiring that everyone get married the best way they can. Take the twenty-seven A men and marry them where they should marry (into C). Next take the sixty B men and marry them into their appropriate class, B, and then marry off the remaining sixty B men wherever they can find wives. The following table gives the actual marriages without brackets and the figures that would apply if you adopted the rule that everyone had to get married enclosed in brackets. They are very close. And the "flow of women" goes as it should: $A \rightarrow B \rightarrow C \rightarrow A$, i.e. marriage in a circle.

TABLE THREE

ACTUAL AND PREDICTED DISTRIBUTION OF PURUM MARRIAGES

		Women of	
	A	B	C
Men of A	(0)	(0)	(27)
	0	1	26
Men of B	(23)	(15)	(22)
	23	16	21
Men of C	(0)	(54)	(0)
	0	52	2

So it appears that generalized exchange can take place with small as well as with large populations, provided you use common sense and do not require that people not marry simply because the rule would be broken.

MATRILATERAL MARRIAGE AND THE SYSTEM OF MEANING

The systems often give rise to a system of meanings in which dualism appears. It's as though the whole world were arranged into oppositional sets along the lines of "wife-givers" versus "wife-receivers." Thus, just as we had asymmetries embedded in dualistic systems which were supposedly characterized by reciprocity, so we have dualism embedded in these asymmetric systems—a dualism that pervades local thinking. As Needham has shown using the Purum data, the Berber house and the Purum house are analogous to one another, divided dualistically, but with different symbols, transformed into the social division that accords with wife-givers and wife-takers. And a brief summary of this dualistic symbolism can be adapted from Needham and compared with the Shavante data of Maybury-Lewis.[3]

TABLE FOUR

DUALISTIC CLASSIFICATION SCHEME OF PURUM

Wife-Takers	Wife-Givers
Front	Back
Affines	Kin
Strangers	Family
Inferior	Superior
Female	Male
Mortals	Gods, ancestral spirits
Sun	Moon
Bad death	Good death
Profane	Sacred
Forest	Village
Evil Spirits	Beneficial Spirits

In fact, human beings play with ideas about their cosmological world, illness, sorcery, marriage, the animal world in a consistent and complicated way. They are all tied together, and if I have given the impression that the social symbols take precedence over other kinds of symbols, the reader should remember that this is simply an artificial by-product of the fact that I am writing a book about social organization. "Keeping things straight" does not mean simply keeping social categories straight, important as this is; it means keeping the world straight. Some of the ways that human beings do it are, to repeat, reciprocity, preference ordering, restricted exchange between two groups, generalized exchange between a number of groups, and opposition versus ranked symbols. Lévi-Strauss has called all of the systems we have so far discussed in chapters 5 and 6 "elementary systems" because they are closed up, things are well ordered, and there are positive rules that attach to marriage and to symbolic exchange in general.[4] They can be compared to the systems we next consider, where the world is not so well ordered, where "probability" rather than determinate rule systems operate. Here we will find that preference ordering is carried out to its fullest extent, transitivity reigns, as it were, and, as a result, human beings are capable of organizing themselves to the full, using their most powerful metric and its associated properties of ordering and transitivity. I will give two examples: segmentary lineage systems and what I call caste/class systems. A lot of people have objected to my lumping class systems (which are democratic and good since people can move up the system by their own—Horatio Alger—efforts) with caste systems, where a posi-

3. Rodney Needham, *Structure and Sentiment* (Chicago: University of Chicago Press, 1962).
4. Claude Lévi-Strauss, *The Elementary Structures of Kinship* (Boston: Beacon Press, 1969).

tion in a transitive hierarchy is fixed at birth, even though the caste can move up and down, and of course there are profound differences between them. But taking our "Martian" point of view and concentrating on the basic principles of human social organization, they are sufficiently similar to be taken together.

SEGMENTARY LINEAGE SYSTEMS

When the Sunday schoolteacher asked in his parson's voice whether all the children in the study group liked the Bible, everyone agreed except one child, who stated flatly that he thought it was "okay, but I didn't like all the 'begats'." "Begats" may be tiresome reading to American children, but in many societies in the world they are of primary importance in keeping things straight. Ben Blount, a linguistic anthropologist, got interested in the "begats" and got two elderly Luo (East African) gentlemen, who were renowned for their knowledge in such matters, and set them to sorting things out with a tape recorder to record their ruminations. It took about two days to sort the whole thing out, but they came to a rough and ready agreement and it became apparent that the model they were working with was a kind of pyramid model. "In the beginning there was the founding ancestor of the tribe, and he had three brothers, and they begat...who begat...who begat...until today we can see the children of the founding father, their living descendants in our villages." The notion of an *apical ancestor*, a founding father from whom the tribe is descended and sometimes named, and the tracing of relationships through his sons and his sons' sons down the generations produces an arrangement of households on the ground in which everyone traces their relationship to

everyone else (if they want to spend two days with an anthropologist and a tape recorder) through males. This is called *agnatic* descent and is distinguished from *uterine* descent, the less common form of descent reckoning, which is through females.

There is a common confusion that we must dispel. I just stated that Blount's Luo informants traced relationships through males: does that mean that anyone with whom one is related via a female is not kin to one? No, and no again. Kinship is always, everywhere *bilateral*. My maternal uncle in the most strictly agnatic (patrilineal) society is a very important relative to me. Most assuredly as well are my mother's parents. And I will have kinship terms for them. But when group membership is being sorted out, in a patrilineal system it is the male links that matter. Women belong to their brothers' groups, but sometimes transfer to their husband's groups over the period of their marriage. But sometimes they don't; they keep their maiden name, as we would say.

Do *we* have agnatic descent groups? No again, even though names pass down the patriline. We have *cognatic* kinship and *kindreds,* which is the anthropological word for kinship groups that include kinfolk from both mother's and father's side. Mostly we have "relatives," or that is what Americans say, and we don't regard them as any kind of well-defined group, the way we might regard our mess mates in the Navy or the gang we hung out with as adolescents.

A pyramid of descent groups can be easily diagrammed and understood, if we remember that each male (triangle) represents a number of generations of "begats" and that those two Luo gentlemen were not performing magnificent mnemonic feats, but rather were arguing how things ought to have been so as to get them politically,

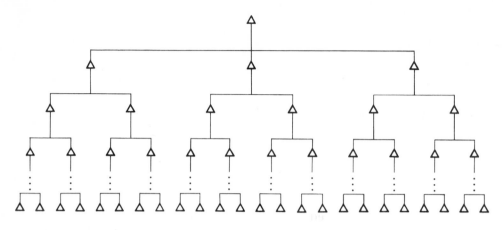

Figure 6. Segmentary Lineage System

socially, and economically where they were today consistent with an agnatic ideology. (Genealogies are negotiated, as well!)

In the Middle East, where lineages are patrilineal, endogamous, and important, they talk about the oppositions between segments (the bottom, living, "flesh and blood" triangles) and about building alliances as follows: "It's me and my brothers against my close cousins," and "me and my brothers and my close cousins against my distant cousins," and "all of us against the outsider."

To get back to our principles: transitive preference ordering is weaker in segmentary systems than it is in caste/class systems, *unless* there is primogeniture (privileges of greater prestige accorded to the first-born son), in which case the preference ordering principle is very strong. In the Marquesan Islands, this principle held, according to Linton, and informants recounted the arrogance of the first born child of five years of age ordering his parents out of the house and keeping them out for the major part of the day.[5] In some systems there is an idea of a royal lineage with cadet lines, and the closer you are to

the royal lineage, the higher your prestige. In this system the highest prestige is accorded to the person who is the first born of the royal lineage. (Children like these get to lock you out of your house!)

But even where primogeniture is not important, there is preference ordering and it is based on the individual. Every individual has to marry outside his own lineage (and usually his mother's lineage, too). In marriage, then, he takes distant blood relatives (consanguines) and converts them into close affines ("in-laws"). Every child born to the marriage will have matrilateral relatives under agnatic descent, just as a child born into a group that uses *uterine* descent (i.e., through women) will have patrilateral relatives.

Preference ordering is based on closeness. There is an implicit moral scale that underlies segmentary systems, whereby obligations recede with distance from the group. If my brother's son won't help me, then I am a real political nonentity because he is about as close as you can get. But if

5. See the account in A. Kardiner, *The Individual and His Society* (New York: Columbia University Press).

my fourth cousin will help me, then I have obviously manipulated the social system so as to put myself in a powerful position. *Blood money* is a nice instance of the moral scale. If you murder someone within your immediate family (including brothers and brothers' sons), then you are guilty of a "special crime" that does not involve revenge or the payment of blood money.[6] It is settled within the close family. But once outside the arena of immediate kinfolk, blood money is paid in decreasing proportion to the distance between the groups. This kind of ego-centered preference ordering is a powerful moral principle that can serve to activate political alliances (pity the poor tribesman from another group who murders a member of a segmentary system and finds the victim's whole clan, or tribe, after him!), and it can keep very large numbers (up to a million) people ordered.

So far as the system of meaning is concerned, preference and closeness are combined to order the cosmological system and the economic spheres as well. Some East African cattleherders know the lineages of their cattle at least as well as they know their own. And in a series of studies of these people in East Africa, Evans-Pritchard and Godfrey Lienhardt have shown how heaven and earth operate on the same set of ideas. Ancestor worship is commonly found in such societies, emphasizing the pyramidal structure.

In two contrasting cases, the matrilineal Plateau Tonga, who regard their village as primary sources of identity, and the patrilineal Lugbara (both African tribes), one can readily see the complex relationships between the social order and the cosmological (remembering that the cosmological order is only one aspect of the semiotic system). Elizabeth Colson, who studied the Tonga, notes that the beliefs in *muzimu* ("ancestral spirits") reproduce the social order. Each person in Tonga is affiliated with a matrilineal group and receives an ancestral spirit from it. But since inheritance goes down that matriline, so does the ancestral spirit when one dies. And since the members of the same matrilineal group are considered to be equivalent, the *muzimu* of anyone in the line can affect the lives of anyone else. Similarly, the importance of the household is reflected in the beliefs that (1) one cannot become an ancestral spirit when one dies unless one has formed a proper household; (2) the absence of local shrines attests to the dispersal of the matrilineal kinfolk in different villages; and (3) the authority of the husband over the wife turns up as the dominance of his *muzimu* over hers in ritual invocations.[7]

In Middleton's analysis, a nice contrast appears because the Lugbara have a patrilineal system in which the dead ancestors and ghosts are felt to have malignant effects upon the living. Further, it is uncertain whether the elders are living or dead.[8] And as Mary Douglas has pointed out, where ambiguities occur, there danger lies, and it comes as no surprise to note that the elders are regarded as potential witches or sorcerers.[9] "Keeping things

6. If you think that decriminalization of murder within the family is strange, you should see and understand the attitude of prison guards towards persons who have murdered close kin. They are regarded as harmless, "good prisoners doing good time," and given preferential treatment within the prison. They are the opposite of those who murdered somebody "on the street," who are referred to as psychopaths or "badasses," and placed under maximum security.

7. Elizabeth Colson, "Ancestral Spirits and Social Structure among the Plateau Tonga," in *International Archives of Anthropology* (Oxford: Oxford University Press, 1954), pp. 21-68.

8. John Middleton, *Lugbara Religion: Ritual and Authority among an East African People* (London: International African Institute, 1954).

9. Mary Douglas, *Purity and Danger* (London: Routledge and Kegan Paul, 1966) and idem, "Pollution" in Davis L. Sills, ed., *International Encyclopedia of the Social Sciences* (New York: Macmillan, 1968).

straight" in Tonga meant aligning heaven and earth, whereas in Lugbara it meant creating a category of evil beings, neither living nor dead. The social system and the system of meaning are in contact with each other, sometimes opposed, sometimes transformed, sometimes replicated, but always themselves a system of meanings, as well as the arrangement of warm bodies in space.

CASTE-CLASS SYSTEMS

In segmentary systems, transitive preference ordering occurs in the form of rules that relate social segments. But there is a profound difference between preference ordering in segmentary societies, and the same in caste/class systems: the first is ego-centered, or symmetrical, while the second is society-wide and asymmetrical. In the segmentary system, if you are my fourth cousin, then I am obligated to aid and assist you in a fourth-cousinly way and pay a comparatively small amount of blood money to your kinfolk when I murder you; and the same holds for you when you are thinking about me.

When society-wide preference ordering takes place, then the problem of *pariah* groups (that is, low-class or low-caste groups) is created because the orderings are both transitive and agreed to by all members of society, and so if A⟩B and B⟩C, then A⟩C, and that's that. None of this business of the brain surgeon's son being honored to marry the sanitation man's daughter. In the words of the old English hymn:

> The rich man in his castle,
> The poor man at his gate,
> God made the high and lowly,
> And ordered their estate.

Or, as Rose, the chamber maid in the Edwardian soap opera "Upstairs-Downstairs" said to the socialist preachments of the daughter of the house: "Would be a funny world if all the people were mixed up, wouldn't it?" Funny, perhaps, but certainly possible, because there are other ways of ordering people and groups than in hierarchically ranked categories. But the fact remains that transitive hierarchies are very powerful ways of organizing large numbers of people in complex and large-scale societies.

CLASS SYSTEMS

Little need be said about class systems. Every reader of English has participated in them. It seems strange that when Lloyd Warner pointed out some fifty years ago that democratic America had a class system, there were some people who were shocked or at least feigned shock, but the pretense was rather similar to the Victorian woman who heard the word "leg" spoken in a drawing room, instead of the proper form, "limb." Even Victorian drawing room ladies were aware of the existence of legs and it requires very upper-class status in this country and England to be unaware of the workings of the class system.

In America, we have a class/caste system, the caste aspects of which seem to be slowly breaking down with the growing acceptance by Americans of heterogeneity of culture within the country so as to include blacks, *chicanos*, American Indians, and people of different cultural heritages as being just as "American" as anyone else. The older idea of the *melting pot*, into which everyone was dipped until they emerged fully American, has been slowly given up in favor of the idea that people should express themselves in the fullness of their own integrity, even though the styles of different Americans may be quite different. But, this is a comparatively recent phenomenon and we really cannot foretell its future success or failure.

It is sobering, however, to remember how recent this phenomenon is. Gerald Berreman, as recently as 1959, was able to write an article in which he substituted "low-caste" or "untouchable" into paragraphs about black-white relations in the American South, and found them to be theorems about Indian caste society. Here is an example, translating Dollard's work on caste and class in a southern town:

In simplest terms, we mean by "a sexual gain" the fact that the [high-caste] men, by virtue of their caste position, have access to two classes of women, those of the [high] and [low] castes. The same condition is somewhat true of the [low-caste] women, except that they are rather the objects of the gain than the choosers, though it is a fact that they have some degree of access to [high-caste] men as well as men of their own caste. [Low-caste] men and [high-caste] women, on the other hand, are limited to their own castes in sexual choices.[10]

Berreman was able to make a point-by-point comparison between the caste system of village India and black-white relations in the United States, even to the point of showing that the high-caste rationalizations of the system ("the Negro is happy in his place") with the statements of Brahmin twice-born, upper-caste Indians, and similarly, he noted that low-caste Indian villagers were able to describe shucking and jiving for the man and what that did to one's self-esteem.[11]

Hierarchy runs throughout Western and American thinking. Life is a ladder to be scaled and one doesn't want to be left behind. America is famous for its "progress," which is forward, onward, and upward, all in a straight line, through "linear" time. (Some peoples think of time as recurring in cycles-within-cycles, which neatly cancels out the past-present-future distinction, since the past is the future. But we see time as a straight line, and our lives are devoted to self-improvement and the improvement of our lives.) We can preference order the most extraordinary things, as many of our psychological tests show. Which is redder, a house or a father? A father, of course: ask any five-year-old child. A number of useful psychological tests are based on our (should I call it natural?) tendency to rank order things. Progressive teachers are told not to make invidious comparisons among children, since it damages their self-esteem and confidence in themselves. Instead they should say, "Why, Mary, you are a better reader than Johnny, but Johnny draws better than you!" From this the child learns that there are a lot of scales or dimensions that he or she can be measured on. The debates over IQ tests reflect not only the naive faith that people have in this stuff called "intelligence," but also (in my view) a compelling need that Americans have to produce a single scale on which they can preference order their whole society.

And, as I mentioned, as an inevitable consequence, pariah groups, or untouchables, or low-class people are created and subsequently endowed with all manner of bad characteristics. It is normal for low-class people to be criminal in nature, as it is for "outsiders" to be witches among the Zapotec. In our research in prisons, this point was made to me by a black rehabilitation officer who pointed out that one of the things that he has to teach young prisoners is that they are not necessarily "bad people" despite the fact that they are in jail. The American "ladder" system has put them into a pariah group and has imputed all manner of evil characteristics to them which are not necessarily true at all. They are bad because they are low-caste, and

10. Gerald Berreman, "Caste in India and the United States," American Journal of Sociology 4 (1959).
11. Ibid.

being low-caste is the consequence of the way society is put together and not necessarily their personal morality.

Transitive preference orderings are powerful devices for organizing large numbers of people into complex relations. But it overrides complexity too, in the sense that it demands a single measuring stick for the whole society. One of the motives behind the slogan "do your own thing" was to attack the transitivity principle. If you are doing your own thing, and valuing it highly and are content with it, and I can honestly respect you for it, then I am rejecting preference ordering in favor of reciprocity and rejecting a single dimension of judgment for multiple dimensions. I am rejecting the model of caste and class in favor of the model of kinship.

CASTE IN INDIA

Preference ordering is carried to a logical extreme in the caste system of South India. Every person is born into the caste, or *jati*, of his father, and *jatis* are ranked. There is a general consensus in Indian communities on the relative rankings of the *jatis*. The rankings vary from community to community, but there is consensus about the major categories. From Brahmin to Untouchable, everyone has their place and their duty (*karma*). Despite the fact that contemporary peoples are living in the age of Kali Yuga, when impurity, disorder, and sin occur, and the rains do not come on time, every person has their place in the society and achieves *dharma*, perfect orderliness in the universe, through the medium of perfect service (*karma*).

The whole universe is ranked in such a way that at a different time *dharma* would be achieved. Animals are ranked: first the cow, the repository of the spirits, then tigers and lions and, finally, sheep and dogs. Each jati is associated with ranked gods in the universe: the high-caste, twice-born Brahmin is associated with the high gods, Shiva and Parvati, while the lower castes are associated with more bumptious and less spiritual gods.

Food is ranked and linked with pollution and purity. High jatis are vegetarian, low are meat-eaters, and the very low even eat beef. At the bottom of the hierarchy are the Untouchable castes, which I discussed earlier.

The hierarchy is saturated with symbols, and these symbols are exchanged. The most tangible form that exchange takes is the exchange of services. The Barber caste is responsible for shaving and cutting the hair of all people, the Goldworker subcaste is an itinerant caste and goes from place to place carrying out its karma. The Brahmin caste has the high duty of keeping the temples and maintaining purity in the community.

One symbol that is not exchanged is spouses. One marries within one's own jati, preferably a person who is known not to be a "brother" or "sister," that is, not a person of one's own patrilineage, but rather a person whose status as "potential spouse" is well known: a close relative such as father's sister's daughter (not one's own lineage, but that of my father's sister's husband), mother's brother's daughter, or, perhaps best of all, elder sister's daughter. And even in the place where one would most expect to find reciprocity and equality—marriage—hypergamous marriage rules are found. A man should marry a woman of lower status than himself. (We will discuss the reasons in the next chapter). Here, in South India, hierarchy pervades every aspect of the social and symbolic order. Everything in its place, and a place for everything; this is dharma, and will happen at the end of the age of Kali Yuga, just as it was before.

CASTE/CLASS SOCIETIES AND THEIR REVERSALS

I was at pains to point out that in societies characterized by dualism and symmetric exchange, asymmetry was to be found just as symmetry and dualism appeared in systems of asymmetric exchange. Every social order seems to have its opposite coded within itself, just as every particle in the universe supposedly corresponds to its antithesis: the antiparticle.

In America, and all class systems, we have the Horatio Alger myth. It is proper and virtuous to raise one's station, to try to get to the top. For this reason we seem to endow wealth and success with moral value, despite our knowledge that it takes a fair amount of immorality and selfishness to reach the top. Similarly we endow the unsuccessful with moral turpitude and attribute their condition to sin. Poverty is failure, failure is reprehensible; striving is good, and success is virtue. All of these feelings are premised on the existence of a ladder of classifications up which one may climb. The purpose of the government's social programs is not to tamper with the (sacred) ladder, but to enable all people to have a crack at climbing it. That done, devil take the hindmost.

In India the caste, or ladder system, is securely anchored in thought and ordered symbol. No man may rise into a higher caste, although by great economic and political efforts the whole jati may rise, and the individual may rise in esteem by raising his standards of purity. Instead of a Horatio Alger myth, we find a reincarnation myth. People who have performed their karma, no matter how low their jati, will be reborn into a higher jati. The hardworking servant who is loyal to his master and pursues the way of dharma will be reborn a prince. But pity the lazy shepherd who abused his animals; he will be reborn as a donkey to be abused and kicked.

Here, as in all societies, social symbols are created and then denied, transformed into their opposite, and extended into space. In short, the world of social symbols is a creation of the rich imagination of the human mind. Society, as Lévi-Strauss said, is "a good vehicle for thought," a system of symbols that can be opposed, transformed, replicated, and regenerated in a myriad of ways to give meaning and richness to our daily strivings and collective life.[12]

For Further Reading

Douglas, Mary (1973) *Natural Symbols*. New York. Vintage Books.
———. (1970) *Purity and Danger*. Baltimore, Md., Penguin Books. Both these books deal with the problem of ambiguity in symbolic systems, and talk about how danger lies when symbols become confused, or ill-defined.
Marriott, McKim (ed.) (1955) *Villiage India*. Chicago, University of Chicago Press. A set of classic studies of village life in India, by recognized scholars of the area.

Bibliography

Lévi-Strauss, C. 1969. *The Elementary Structures of Kinship*. Boston: Beacon Press.

Needham, Rodney 1968. *Structure and Sentiment*. Chicago: University of Chicago Press.

12. Lévi-Strauss, *The Elementary Structures of Kinship*.

7 | Ecology and Social Organization

So far I have been talking about people manipulating social categories, sorting things out together, and giving meaning, *social* meaning, to the world around them, linking their thoughts about who they are and who other people are with the natural and cosmological world. But, as the saying goes, people do not live on social categories alone, they have to work for a living. We have to *situate* social organization in a setting, a landscape, and discuss the relationships between the way people organize themselves and how they get food onto the table and into their children's mouths.

This is an extensive topic of growing interest to anthropologists, agronomists, economists, and every person who is interested in preventing world starvation and averting a breakdown of national cultural institutions at the same time. I cannot possibly do more than suggest some of the issues involved.

HUMAN BEINGS ARE RATIONAL?

A distinguished entomologist, in being granted an honorary degree from Harvard University, was cited for his great work on the social life of ants and other insects, which had proved "that there were other forms of social life that could be intricately organized *without* the use of reason!" This chapter is going to be devoted to the opposite of that proposition: human beings, in my view, *are* rational despite evidence to the contrary, and it is the anthropologist's job to discover the forms that rationality takes in different social and cultural situations. I am going to have to introduce a number of technical terms to display what I mean, and then I will discuss three case studies that display what I think is convincing evidence that human beings are rational.

RATIONAL IS OPTIMAL

"Rationality" has a strict meaning in this context: it means that human beings allocate their resources (technological and personal) in an *optimal* way, or in more colloquial terms, "they do the best they can with what they got, to get the most out of life." *Optimal* is the technical term that means "the best they can." "Getting the most out of life" can be put back into jargon by stating that given the constraints under which human beings operate in all societies, they attain their goals in an effective and efficient manner. "Their goals" are important, because so often we think of words like "efficient" and "optimal" as indicating that man is like a laboring ant minimizing wasted time and producing maximum output so as to optimize some return, usually monetary in nature. And that is patently false. No person anywhere does that. But some work, including some that I have carried out with my colleagues, indicates that if one understands the goals that people have in life, one (what goes into and defines the "pursuit of happiness," for example) finds that on the average, people are very intelligent in pursuing the goals that they define in their own cultural terms, given socially defined priorities and their individual quirks.

WHAT IS A CONSTRAINT?

People everywhere are constrained in their activities. Their level of technology is one constraint. North American Indians were sitting (and hunting) on an immense pool of oil, but they never exploited it because, first, they didn't need it, and second, they didn't have a technology that would enable them to extract it. The prototype of the steam engine was invented by an unknown engineer at the court of the tyrant Hiero of Syracuse (a city-state of ancient Italy), but was never developed because there was no *perceived* need for it, the kindred technology for its exploitation had not yet been invented, and so it passed beneath their eyes. The wheel was invented by the ancient civilizations of Mesoamerica, but only used on children's toys since human bearers in those mountainous regions were more efficient than wheeled vehicles. *Technology* constitutes one set of constraints on human effectiveness.

ENVIRONMENTAL CONSTRAINTS

There are two kinds of environmental constraints; or rather, two ways of thinking about the environment: the *effective environment* and the *perceived environment*. The effective environment is the "real world" environment that agronomists, meterologists, ecologists, and scientists study: the set of *relationships* between human beings and their environment that have "real" consequences. If it doesn't rain, crops will not grow without irrigation. If the soil is rocky and hilly it will be unsuitable for cereal agriculture on a large scale. If cattle are raised in certain swampy areas, they will die of trypanosomiasis, and that's that. Those are the facts that scientists know about, and they define the limits of productive success just as effectively as does the level of technological development. But there is another environment that is important, particularly to the anthropologist who studies it more closely than anyone else: that is, the *perceived* environment, or the way human beings think about their setting and its limitation so as to construct adequate *strategies* for getting food on the table. Sometimes these beliefs coincide with the effective environment, but sometimes they don't. The Tsembaga tribesmen, whom Roy Rappaport studied, believe that there are evil spirits in the lowlands which forbid human habitation. This coincides with the scientific knowledge that below 3500 feet the area is infested with anopheles mosquitoes, which carry malaria (unbeknownst to the Tsembaga), which indeed makes the area uninhabitable. But sometimes the perceived environment does not jibe with the effective environment. So far as it is known, rain dances do not bring rain, even though they summon the spirits that control the rain. And the Zapotec Indians believe that their land is best used for the raising of maize, when the U.N. agronomists and our project's work in some Zapotec communities indicate that the land would be much better used in raising livestock. When I make the claim that people are rational, I am making a relatively weak claim because I am saying that they are rational so far as they exploit the perceived environment, rather than the effective environment.

TWO KINDS OF RATIONALITY

We have to be aware of two kinds of rationality: *individual rationality* and *collective rationality*. Individual rationality refers to the behavior of individual production and consumption units, which can be nuclear families, matrifocal households, kinship groups, lineages, joint families, or whatever. Collective rationality refers to the welfare of the whole social group. It is almost always the case that were everyone to be individually rational, maximizing like crazy and ignoring everyone else, that the society would fall apart. Collective rationality is the study of the constraints that exist when people "decide" to live together and cooperate, exploiting their perceived environment as best they can, mixing their strategies according to their means, skills, wealth, and the like so as to achieve the highest level of welfare for the whole group. This is a very difficult and complex study, usually carried out by "welfare economists," and we will use the work of Morgan Maclachlan to show how it works in a South Indian community.

ARE HUMAN BEINGS REALLY RATIONAL?

I will further abridge my claim for human rationality by stating that human beings are not completely rational, in the sense of being supermanagerial wizards in pushing themselves as far as the technological, environmental, and social constraints will permit. In microeconomics we talk about the "optimal frontier," which represents the very best that people can do, given their goals and the constraints on fulfilling these goals. People do not sit on their optimal frontier. They may sometimes achieve it, but on the whole they *approximate* it. Another jargony way

of stating the same is to say that human beings do not *satisfice,* i.e., they don't take the very first solution they can come up with that will meet their needs, as some people have claimed. They do much better than that. They approximate the optimal condition.

THREE CASE STUDIES

I am going to use three case studies to illustrate these points. The first, the Tsembaga, studied by Rappaport, illustrates the relationship between social groups and the effective environment; the second, the Zapotec, illustrates the relationships between the goals that people have (cultural definition of the "pursuit of happiness") and the constraints of the perceived environment, and technology. The third will deal with the problem of the welfare economist: the relationship between the ways the rules of marriage, kinship, residence, and descent operate to solve the problem of optimizing collective welfare.

THE TSEMBAGA[1]

The Tsembaga number about 200 people, organized in five patrilineal clans, who reside in the New Guinea Highlands in a forested area of 3.2 miles that ranges in altitude from 2700 to 7200 feet. They subsist mainly on root crops: sweet potatoes and taro in the main, but also yams, bananas, manioc, and pandanus. Rappaport looks at the Tsembaga to see how four factors interrelate: trophic requirements (i.e., enough food on the table), subsistence techniques (the technology of garden agriculture and pig raising), war-

1. See, Roy Rappaport, *Pigs for the Ancestors* (New Haven, Conn.: Yale University Press, 1968). I have also been aided in my understanding of the New Guinea materials by papers and conversations with Denise O'Brien, Lorraine Sexton, and Andrew P. Vayda.

fare, and ritual behavior. The *effective environment* sets the limits on the productivity of horticultural and pig husbandry. Rappaport analyzes the *carrying capacity* of the Tsembaga lands, which is a way of calculating how many people could be supported by their environment, given their requirements, and finds it more than adequate. From the point of view of the Tsembaga gardener there are major problems with pigs, however. First, since pigs are only eaten during illnesses and ritual occasions they often threaten to overrun the gardens, tearing down the fences around the sweet potato patches and second, they threaten to "eat one out of house and home," since people and pigs subsist on the same diet: sweet potatoes.

Neighbors are, and can be, a problem since every society must maintain its boundaries. In general, the distribution of a people over the landscape, here or anywhere, must be accomplished so as to maintain a fairly healthy distance between the local groups and starvation. (Every traditional society that I and my colleagues have studied seems to ensure that there is a lot of slack in their economy: they are more afraid of disaster, and adjust their agricultural strategies accordingly, than they are eager to exploit their natural and human resources so as to maximize the exploitation of their environment.)

What Rappaport shows is that all these problems, that is (1) the problem of caloric intake; (2) the problem of productivity; (3) the problem of maintaining a balance between the pig population and the human population; and (4) the problem of maintaining proper relationships with one's neighbors, including distribution of people on the ground so as to leave a safety margin between the whole (Maring) tribe (to which the Tsembaga belong) and disaster, are accomplished through ritual and warfare.[2]

Start with the problem of the pig population, recalling that pigs are only eaten when a person is ill or injured or when there is a peace-making ritual at the conclusion of a local conflict. When the pig herd is small, the labor involved in supporting it is minimal because the herd can be fed on the roots that are not fit for human consumption. But when the herd gets large, special plots of sweet potatoes must be planted to feed it. In fact, when the herd was at its maximum size (170 animals), 36 percent of the gardens were planted to feed them. Since the women do most of the work for maintaining the pigs, they complain very much about the size of the herd, and it has to be reduced.

There are two ways of reducing the pig population which will ensure that the trophic requirements of both animals and men will remain well within the carrying capacity of the environment. One can make peace or war. And the second is a requirement for the first (no peace without war). Thus a homicide is committed against a neighboring "enemy" group and vengeance is called for. Skirmishes between the two groups escalate into invasions, which in turn escalate into true warfare and sometimes the dispersal of the whole enemy population. Dispersal occurs infrequently; usually the two sides decide that enough killing has taken place, and they begin the process of reestablishing good relations. At every juncture in this process, and in particular in the process of bringing the two sides together, pigs are required. Pig feasts are held and slowly but surely the pig herd reduces to a size where it can reproduce itself, but where the labor in sustaining it is not excessive, thus eliminating difficulties for the women.

2. There is a story in the profession which attaches to different people at different times, that some anthropologist made the statement that "warfare functions to reduce conflict." This is obvious nonsense. Rappaport is not stating that "warfare is functional, that is, good for the welfare of all," he is saying, "this is how it happens, why it happens, and these are the consequences."

From the point of view of the analyst of population pressure, it can be readily seen that population dispersal can alter the ecological relationship until a new equilibrium is established.

From the point of view of the nutritionist, it can also be seen that the caloric intake of the Tsembaga and their neighbors would not suffice to sustain them in good condition (adequate nutritional status would not be maintained) unless there were these periodic "injections" of high quality protein into the diet which are achieved through the rituals of war and peace and the pig feasts.

The Maring, it need not be added, do not see it this way at all. They are concerned with hate, hostilities, aggression, appeasement of the spirits, the proper respect for taboos, and keeping their women happy, or at least not constantly complaining. They are conscious of some aspects of their effective environment, but far from all. They represent a typecase of how successful adaptation within the effective environment requires the balancing of multiple interacting causes and effects which feed into each other in a complex way so as to effect a human solution to the problems raised by technology and the environment.

THE PERCEIVED ENVIRONMENT AND THE PURSUIT OF HAPPINESS

The reader may have noticed that there was an apparent contradiction in my comments about the Tsembaga and the comments I made earlier about the rationality of human beings. I said that the Tsembaga (like most of the communities and tribes that have been studied) keep well within the carrying capacities of their lands, preferring strategies that would avert disaster (at all costs) to higher risk strategies that would lead to much higher production levels.

How can the Tsembaga be said to be optimal, rational people, then, since they don't dwell on their "optimal frontier"? In a word, I am saying that people can be seen to be operating optimally *only* if you know what they want out of life. Consider the following scene being observed by a missionary, a nutritionist, an agricultural economist, and an anthropologist: a drunken, raggedly dressed Zapotec Indian is sitting in front of his house, which is a bamboo hut that lacks a stick of furniture (except for a transistor radio that the anthropologist gave him for his hard work). The missionary would be disgusted at the low moral condition of the people, and particularly this man, who is clearly neglecting his small children, living in a hovel, subsisting on a barely adequate diet, and not trying to get ahead in the world at all. The nutritionist examines him and finds his nutritional status barely adequate and his children malnourished (though not seriously so: a deficiency of vitamin C seems the only major problem); and the agricultural economist notes that capital formation is being impeded by this man's laziness and his drinking, and besides, he is not even raising the correct crops. And the anthropologist looks at him and says, "Aha, a clear case of formal rationality!" By all the canons of modern economic analysis, this man is acting rationally in his own best interests, so far as constructing and implementing strategies for the "good life" are concerned. (I should add that this is a true case of an individual that we studied over a period of five years with hundreds of hours of interviewing.)

The difference between the anthropologist and the others is that he has tried to understand (1) what the man's goals are in life; (2) how he perceives the best way of obtaining these goals; and (3) how he perceives the potential in his environment, his priorities, and the best way of meeting these priorities.

We take the group's observations in

order: he is drunk, why? It turns out that the anthropologist knows two things that the other three do not: first, the man's eldest son has just come of age and is working full-time for his father on his father's land, and (2) that although the man is drunk, he is also drunk on purpose, the purpose being to join in a ritual which will enable him, for the first time in his life, to form political and economic relationships with his kinfolk via a ritual called (in Spanish) the *cuelga*, where drunkenness is a required mark of respect. This is the first time that the man has had the opportunity to cement these alliances since his eldest son died of yellow fever some four years ago. He is making up for lost time in the necessary fence mending that is so important to social and economic life in a Zapotec community.

"But," says the economist, "why is the man carrying out dry corn farming when my analysis of soils and carrying capacities clearly indicates that he should take his limited amount of capital and invest it in livestock and dairying, sell the corn land, and buy irrigable land where he can raise prime cattle feed (alfalfa)?" The answer is that one of his goals is *security*, and he feels that one of the most important components of security is an adequate corn supply, so that he has enough corn on hand to feed his family tortillas, his pigs maize, and sufficient left over to plant next year. All the villagers feel this way. They are aware (but not nearly as sophisticatedly as the economist) about price fluctuations in dairy produce and meat, and they know that they probably would do better on the average if they went into wholesale dairying, but there are three catches. First, if everyone went into dairy farming there wouldn't be enough irrigable land in the community to grow the feed, so that their profit margins would be correspondingly reduced. (This comes up later when we compare individual versus

collective rationality.) Second, they know that the price of corn can also fluctuate and they would rather stay out of that game and suffer the consequences of changes in the world commodity market of which they know nothing. And third, they avoid risk when they can. There are two farming strategies in the village: one is high-risk/high-payoff, and it means planting early and gambling on the rains coming early and in sufficient abundance so as to yield a very good crop, and low-risk/low-payoff strategies which imply spreading the planting season out over three months, and getting a much smaller return (on the average) but *some* return always. There is one person in the village who plays the first; all the others play the second. For all but one of the villagers, the loss (or "regret") involved in the lost opportunity of growing greater amounts of corn is more than compensated for in the psychological gain in security that they, being very poor by our standards, are so very concerned with.

But, why does he live in that hovel? Why does he eat meat only once a week, and why does he wear those tattered clothes? This one is more tricky. Good diet, particularly a mixed diet that includes a variety of foods, and most importantly fresh fruit and meat, *is* important to the villager. So is dressing well, even though their scrupulously clean clothes look tatterdemalion in the extreme. Housing, diet, and dress contribute to their goal of a good "style of life" which ranks in the middle of their priorities. But the fact is that it isn't *that* important, unless you are very rich (by village standards, have capital assets valued at about U.S. $3,000.00), when one can and does improve dwelling, diet, and dress. But the poorer villagers recognize the desirability of these improvements, and properly and *rationally* eschew them in favor of devoting all their money to maintaining proper social relations, and to corn production.

Our analysis, which was carried out on a computer because we couldn't handle all the calculations by hand, showed that by and large this villager (and others in the same area) were acting rationally, meeting their priorities in the best way they could, given the way they visualized social imperatives and the *perceived* environment.

HINDU PURITANISM AND COLLECTIVE RATIONALITY[3]

Sometimes the people that we study in traditional society cannot understand why we are so stupid: we have our typewriters, tape recorders, cameras, and cars (sometimes), and yet we don't seem to understand the simplest things. "Genealogy," said the village elder of Yavahalli, "doesn't refer to people, it refers to land!" But up to that point in his extensive interviewing, all Maclachlan had heard was talk about brothers-in-law, fathers-in-law, fathers, wives, elder and younger brothers and sisters, and the like. Surely it sounded like a family tree, and they don't have to do with land, they have to do with "relatives," "relations," and "those people whom you cannot choose, but have to get along with." The village elder meant two things: first, he had an agricultural metaphor in mind, because he, like his fellow villagers, believed that although women were fallow fields into which men planted seeds, that heredity followed the male line: rice planted always yields rice, and this is the basis of the patrilineage. Second, he thought that the anthropologist understood that when he was talking about "genealogy," obviously he was concerned with property, inheritance, and how you get people to work together to get the best they can out of what they have. Had he read his Marx, he would have said, "Look, genealogy refers to the social relations or production and the formation of consumption and production units."

The most efficient production unit in Yavahalli is the joint family, a family containing two or more mature, working men. The advantages of having more than one man in the household in an economy based on irrigated agriculture lie in the men's ability to increase the yields on the (limited) amount of land in the family, or, if they are poor, to rent out their labor as an effective solidary package. Thereby the men make themselves more attractive to big landowners than smaller households of one man.

These South Indian villagers often talk about the good times they had in the family when there was enough food, cash, and relative abundance. This period in the life of the family coincides with the maturity of the sons of the household, before they get married. Trouble begins with the marriage of the eldest son and increases as the younger sons demand brides and receive them. The marriages bring trouble of two kinds: first, the women get pregnant and become concerned with raising children and, thus, their economic contribution to the household drops off, and trouble again because the number of mouths to feed increases, and the "per-person" wealth of the family drops correspondingly.

And this in turn can cause more trouble. As another elder stated, "If you want to know why we have all these troubles, it is because in these days no one knows how to behave. All of these families could be so much better off if they stayed together in one house, but the people quarrel and divide into different houses. I don't know

3. This subheading is almost identical with the title of a paper by Morgan Maclachlan called "Notes on the Collective Rationality of Hindu Puritanism," which is one of the few attempts that I know of to carry out a "welfare analysis" of subsistence farmers which includes not just good, solid quantitative data on economics, but also data on marriage rules, kinship, household and group formation, incest, and the other topics that concerned us in the previous chapters.

why. It is certain that a combined house is better, these small houses are not good."

Maclachlan shows in an elaborate economic analysis that the old man is right. There is more to be gained in forming a coalition, whether one is land rich, or land poor, whether you have a lot of dependents, or few dependents.

What about kinship and marriage? (After all, these are the topics that have concerned me in writing this book.) For one thing, marriage is *hypergamous*, that is, women marry into wealthier families than the families in which they were raised. This accomplishes three things: (1) it guarantees that one's beloved sisters and daughters will marry into houses where they will be well cared for; (2) it ensures late marriage for very poor men, thus depressing the number of dependents, and thereby raising per capita income in the household "firms" of the most poverty-stricken; and (3) it ensures that the woman who comes into the household is relatively powerless, and unable to break the coalition of men (brothers) who form the most efficient collective. Of course it would be very desirable if a minimal number of one's sons married. But they, too, have a threat at their disposal—they can withdraw their labor from the collective pool and become "free riders," and that is precisely what happens when parents refuse to arrange a marriage for their son.

But troubles occur, as the old man said, because the wife gains status with increasing age and with the number of children she bears, and she may well start arguing with the other women over the disposal of goods within the collective, "looking out for her own" rather than joining in the utopian ideology (*dharma*) that the older men constantly preach. Quarrels erupt, men are drawn into them; the network of agreements which are phrased in the terms of kinship, marriage, religion, and ethics, but which reflect land and collective welfare, begins to break down; and the elder brother forms a new household and takes his capital out of the firm. The advantages that accrue to the firm because of economies of scale and which were apparently guaranteed by the hypergamous marriage principle are thrown away.

How can one prevent this? One could, I suppose, imagine a community of saints, but it would correspond to no known human group. Or you could arrange it so that the women would get along and acquiesce in the agreements. One way of avoiding conflict is to have a system of marriage that magnifies the chances of the women getting along. This is what the South Indian villagers do. They have an elaborate system of marriage prohibitions and categories of marriageable kin that puts emphasis on the selection of women who will "buy" the household ideology (propaganda) and not split up the collective. The best wife of all would be a poorer daughter of an elder sister. In the patrilineal system, she is not in the lineage (she belongs to her father's lineage), but elder sister is both trusted, beloved, respected, and regarded as a friend, which, as Maclachlan shows, is true of no other relative. Failing this, marry a woman from a reliable group; that is, a group from which wives have been drawn before. This involves relationships of permanent alliance between kin groups, and arranges them in terms of wife-givers, wife-takers. Further, relationships of permanent alliance provide examples of earlier generations who "went along with" the system, and thus puts added moral pressure on the women of this generation to accept their karma and keep the collective together.

But I can conclude, by quoting Maclachlan directly, who summarizes:

The logic of collective action that emerges from the moral order of kinship can be summarized simply:

1. There are advantages to joint action; the problem lies in producing an organization free of the mistrust that leads to division.

2. Given a choice between maximizing solidarity among the men of a household and that of the women, always choose the men. Men dominate the agricultural economy and therefore one can be more easily hurt by an untrustworthy man than an untrustworthy woman. Moreover, as men dominate women, a solidary group of women could control divisive men. Always choose the most trusted men among kinsmen to live with. Therefore live with father, son, or brother.

3. In choosing women, minimize their motives and power to cause trouble. A younger, poorer daughter of a loved sister would be the best choice.[4]

CONCLUSION

These three examples have served to *situate* the ideas about social categories and their meaning that were explored in the previous chapters. Rappaport's study dealt with the whole society's response to the *effective environment*, the relationship between putting the right amount and kind of food on the table, and the dispersal of population and pigs in the landscape. The Zapotec study showed that people in traditional society, far from being the "backward" group some imagine them to be, are in fact acting rationally, if you will only see the way they perceive their goals, their environment, and the constraints on reaching these goals. And finally, Maclachlan showed us that the elaborate system of meanings and symbols that we have called kinship encode the solution to a problem in welfare economics: how to get the best results from cereal agriculture, given a technology that is dominated by an indivisible good (the well), and from the fact that men working together can create more wealth than they can by working alone.

Bibliography

Legesse, Asmaram 1974. *Gada: Three Approaches to the Study of African Society.* New York: Free Press.

Rappaport, Roy 1968. *Pigs for the Ancestors.* New Haven: Yale University Press.

Vayda, Andrew P. 1961. "Expansion and Warfare among Swidden Agriculturalists." *American Anthropologist* 63:346-358.

4. Morgan Maclachlan, "Notes on the Collective Rationality of Hindu Puritanism" (manuscript, Columbia, S.C., University of South Carolina).

8 | Conclusion

One of the things that a lot of students like about anthropology is that it deals with "everything." Even though I restricted the topic to social anthropology, and even more sharply to social organization, it became clear as the book proceeded that one had to understand biological and sociological imperatives, semiotic systems (systems of meaning), technology, environment, and the relationships between them if one was to construct anything close to an adequate account of human beings in traditional societies.

Though (like the Tsembaga) we have our skirmishes, incursions, and invasions in the profession, I think it is true to say that we are all still committed to studying human beings in their total environment, where that environment includes thinking, symbolling, exchanging human beings doing the best they can to get a decent life for themselves, their families, and their communities.

What anthropology teaches us is relevant to our own present-day problems. In effect, anthropologists say, "Look at the variety of ways in which men and women think about themselves, but look at the commonalities in their experience, too. If America and the rest of the world is truly to commit itself to understanding and peaceful relations, the lessons of anthropology will have to be learned and imprinted not just in the minds of our leaders, but also in the minds of all enlightened people. There is no danger in diversity, except that we label it dangerous, and become fearful of it. There is richness in variety. Cultural systems are robust, changing but stable, and we have nothing to fear in change."

On the other hand, cultural systems and systems of social organization are complex. The way we organize is affected by and affects the way we think, and the way we govern is but a sign of the way we commit ourselves to a set of values and priorities. Meanings attach to all that we do collectively. These meanings may be paradoxical, but paradox is a feature of all systems of meaning, even including that most rigorous system of meaning of all: mathematics. But even the paradoxes have a coherence, even diversity has an underlying commonality, even individual strivings must and can only be given meaning through the mediation of other people.

Life without meaning is a psychotic's nightmare. Life without understanding of the human experience in its richness and variegation is troubled. Life with an understanding of oneself gained from an understanding of the ways of other people is difficult, because we have to give up many of the things that we complacently took for granted when we assumed that our way was the best way, and that people like us were the better people.

There is a condition called "reverse culture shock" that all anthropologists experience, sometimes called the "shock of reentry." It refers to the mixed emotions that an anthropologist has when he or she returns from the field. I recall crossing the border after a year spent with the Zapotec, turning on the car radio and listening to the broadcast of a space shot. It was incredible, not just because I had stepped out of a seventeenth-century technology into an advanced twentieth-century technology, but because of all the "garbage" that went along with it. The space shot was "brought to us" by soap, detergent, underarm body sprays, toothpaste, and all manner of technological devices that protected Americans from dirt and smell. My wife and I began to laugh and then got quite hysterical and completely ignored the space shot in

favor of a fascination for the way that one civilization had tried to veil the conditions of life which were so taken for granted in the culture that we had just left. The anthropologist is called to exotic places he or she never really leaves. It is an experience which is denied to most people and leaves one never quite the same. In some sense we remain marginal to our own culture, just as we were never truly able to penetrate and become full members of the culture we were studying. It is not quite what my friend said when he defined anthropologists as "people who reject their own culture . . .just before their own culture rejects them," but it is an experience that leaves one changed. I have tried to include you in this experience in this book.

Glossary

Agnatic descent—Descent reckoned through males. It is the same as patrilineal descent. *(Cf. uterine descent and bilateral descent)*.

Apical Ancestor—The "Founding Parent" of a lineage.

Bilateral Cross-Cousin Marriage—The system of marriage in which you choose a spouse from a class that is defined as *both* "mother's brother's daughter" *and* "father's sister's daughter."

Bilateral Descent—Descent reckoned through males and females. *(Cf. agnatic descent and uterine descent)*.

Bint 'Amm Marriage—Patrilateral parallel cousin marriage as practiced in the Middle East. (A patrilateral parallel cousin is the child of one's father's brother.)

Circular Connubium—Marriage in a circle. Sometimes called *asymmetric alliance,* sometimes called *matrilateral cross-cousin marriage.*

Constrain—To have an effect on, to set limits on. *(Cf. determine)*.

Cross cousin—A mother's brother's child, or a father's sister's child.

Cultural Relativism—The notion that one cannot compare cultures and say that one is better than another.

Cultural Units—The ideas that a society has and uses to recognize events. They can be conscious or unconscious; they can be expressed in the spoken language, but need not be.

Determine—To have a definitive effect on, so that there is only one result. *(Cf. constrain)*.

Dualism—The cultural practice of defining symbols in pairs or opposites.

Dyadic Relation—A relationship between two people or two groups.

Effective Environment—The environment as scientifically studied and measured by physicists, agronomists, nutritionists, meteorologists, and so on. *(Cf. perceived environment)*.

Endogamous Rule—(Or rule of endogamy). The rule that states how distant a person may be (or how different) and still be a potential spouse.

Exogamous Rules—(Or rule of exogamy). The rule that states how close (or how similar) a person may be and still be a potential spouse.

Fraternal Polyandry—The cultural practice that favors the marriage of a woman to more than one man who must be brothers.

Genetic Father—The man who actually engaged in the act of sexual intercourse that led to the conception of a particular child.

Genetic Mother—The woman who actually engaged in the act of sexual intercourse which led to the conception of a particular child.

Genetrix—The woman who is socially recognized to have borne the child.

Genitor—The man who is socially recognized to have "fathered" the child, however "fathering" be defined in any particular society.

Group Marriage—The (rare) practice of a number of men being married to a number of women.

Homogamy—The cultural practice of marrying someone like yourself: from your own group, class, caste.

Hypergamous Marriage Rule—A rule that states that one's wife's group is of lower status than one's own group. Equally, that one's husband's group is of higher status than one's own.

Hypogamous Marriage Rule—A rule that states that one's wife's group is of higher status than one's own. Equally, that one's husband's group is of lower status than one's own.

Incest Taboo—The rule, found in all human groups, that there is a class of people of opposite sex with whom one may not have sexual intercourse.

Mater—The woman who is socially recognized to be the "mother" of a particular child.

Matrifocal Family—A family made up of a mother and her children. (Sometimes, wrongly, called "absent-father" families).

Matrilineage—A social group recruited on the basis of one's relationships through women.

Matrilineal Extended Family—A family made up of a couple, their married daughters (and grandchildren by these daughters), and their unmarried children of both sexes.

M'Naughten Rules—The British rules of jurisprudence that state that a person must know the difference between right and wrong at the time of the commission of a crime in order to be judged guilty of that crime.

Monogamy—The cultural practice that favors a single spouse for both males and females.

Multifinality—Having many results or outcomes.

Nuclear Family—The family consisting of a socially defined mother, father, and children.

Optimal—Doing the best one can given one's resources, technology, and quirks.

Overdetermination—Having many causes.

Parallel Cousin—One's father's brother's child or one's mother's sister's child.

Pater—The person who is socially recognized to be the "father" of a particular child.

Patrilineage—A social group recruited on the basis of one's relationships through males.

Patrilineal Extended Family—A family consisting of a couple, their married sons (and grandchildren by these sons), and their unmarried children of both sexes.

Perceived Environment—The environment as it is thought of by the people who live in it.

Polygyny—The cultural practice that favors the marriage of a man with more than one wife.

Polyandry—The cultural practice that favors the marriage of a woman with more than one husband.

Rationality—(1) Individual Rationality:

The efficient allocation of resources by a single person or a simple production and consumption unit (like a household). (2) Collective Rationality: The efficient allocation of resources over a whole community so that community-wide welfare is favorably affected.

Recidivism Rate—The rate at which convicted offenders are found guilty of subsequent offenses.

Semiotics—The study of meaning systems or codes.

Sibling—A brother or sister.

Sororal Polygyny—The practice that favors the marriage of a man to more than one wife who must be sisters.

Teknonymy—The practice of tracing kinship through one's children.

Uterine Descent—Descent reckoned through females. (The same as matrilineal descent.) (Cf. *agnatic descent*, and *bilateral descent.*)

Wolf Children—Children who have been brought up in total or near-total isolation.

Index

INDEX
Continued

Gestapo, 7
Gough, Kathleen, 20, 27
Gusii, the, 26

Hugo, Victor, 8
hypergamy, 42, 61
hypogamy, 42

Ik, the, 7, 19, 28
illegitimacy, 22
incest, 24:
   nuclear, 15
   taboo, 14, 15, 17, 18
individual, the, 6
I.B.M., 4

jati, 52
Jones, James, 22

Kadar, the, 26
Kardiner, Abram, 48
karma, 52
Kaufman, Irving, 16, 17
kinship terminology:
   Shavante, 36

Legesse, Asmaram, 62
LeVine, Robert, 25, 26
Lévi-Strauss, Claude, 18, 46, 53
Lienhardt, G., 49
Lindzey, Gardner, 17
Linton, Ralph, 48
Luckman, Thomas, 13
Lugbara, the, 49
Luo, the, 47

Maccoby, Eleanor, 12
Maclachlan, Morgan, 56, 60
Malinowski, Bronislaw, 16
marriage, 23:
   American, 29
   asymmetric alliance and, 42
   bilateral cross-cousin, 37
   bint 'amm, 30
   cowife hostility and, 25
   divorce and, 25
   generalized exchange and, 42
   homogamous, 25, 29
   hypergamous, 42, 52, 61
   hypogamous, 42
   matrilateral cross-cousin, 42-43
   monogamous, 23
   politics and, 35
   polyandrous, 24
   polygynous, 23, 25
   Shavante, 35

Marriott, McKim, 53
Mapuche, the, 43-44
mater, 21, 24, 25
Maybury-Lewis, David, 34, 35, 39
Middleton, John, 49
M'Naughten rules, 8, 9
Moynihan, Daniel P., 22
Murdock, George Peter, 26, 27

Nayar, the, 20
Needham, Rodney, 46, 53
Neel, J. V., 17, 18
Nuremberg doctrine, 9

Oedipal conflict, 15, 23
opposition:
   Berber house and, 33
   Purum cosmology and, 46
   Shavante social, 33
   See also dualism and binarism.
Ornstein, Robert B., 13

pariah group, 42, 50, 51
pater, 21, 24, 25
patrilineage:
   marriage within, 31
   relations between, 35
Peck, Alice, 16, 17
Popper, Karl, 7
preference ordering, 44-53
progress, 1
Purum, the, 44

Radcliffe-Brown, A. R., 5
Rappaport, Roy, 55, 56
rationality, 54-62:
   collective, 60
   individual versus collective, 56
Raven, P. H., 14
reality, 12
Ryan, W., 22

Sanford, Nevitt, 6
Schneider, D. M., 18, 20
Segner, Leslie, 16
Selby, H. A., 9, 13
semiology, 3
semiotics, 3
Service, E. R., 5
Sharanahua, the, 38, 43
Shavante, the, 34, 36, 43
Siskind, Janet, 38, 39
structural functionalism, 3
symbols, 13, 29:
   Berber house and, 33
   Shavante oppositions and, 36
   women and, 33